W9-AGU-422

THE SIEGE OF PARIS, 1870–1871

DC312
KM
1950

The Siege of Paris,
1870-1871

A POLITICAL AND SOCIAL HISTORY

Melvin Kranzberg

AMHERST COLLEGE

CORNELL UNIVERSITY PRESS

Ithaca, New York, 1950

NOV 1962

76498

Copyright 1950 by Cornell University

Cornell University Press

London: Geoffrey Cumberlege

Oxford University Press

PRINTED IN THE UNITED STATES OF AMERICA BY THE
VAIL-BALLOU PRESS, INC., BINGHAMTON, N.Y.

TO THE MEMORY OF MY FATHER

Preface

To the general reader, the siege of Paris is probably best known through Arnold Bennett's *The Old Wives' Tale*, wherein the author describes in humdrum fashion the ordinary lives of the ordinary citizens during the siege and thereby gives credence to his own claim that it was not a "dramatic, spectacular, thrilling, ecstatic affair." To the student of French history, likewise, the siege of Paris appears lacking in interest, and it has been relegated to a minor role as a military episode in the Franco-Prussian War, with its significance for subsequent developments in France completely overshadowed by the Commune of Paris, which took place shortly thereafter.

Yet, a closer study of the siege, especially of its political and social aspects, belies the views of both Mr. Bennett and the ordinary student of French history. While there may have been no heroic military exploits or displays of great political acumen, the siege of Paris brought out dramatic and spectacular qualities in the lives of the inhabitants of the French capital, and the social and political developments which accompanied it, though hitherto neglected, were of decisive importance for subsequent happenings in France.

This book is intended to be more than a mere chronicle of

political events or a case study of the impact of a siege on the life of a great city, interesting as these might be. Since the object of social history is not only to relate and integrate facts dealing with the various aspects of man's life, but also to shed light on the interpretation of his subsequent actions, I have tried to point out the connection between the social and political aspects of life in besieged Paris and their effects upon the outbreak of the Commune, which occurred two months later. Whether or not I have succeeded in these tasks is, of course, for the reader to decide.

Sources for the study of the siege are abundant, but they must be used with great caution. Most of them were written so close to the event, when emotions were still stirred by what had happened, that they lack perspective and are apt to be unreliable. This is especially true of the German and French works dealing with the siege, so it has been necessary to use the accounts of neutral observers to check the extreme views of the partisans. In the case of French works particularly, we must be alive to any perversions of historical evidence caused by the strong feelings aroused by the class struggle which followed close on the siege.

Materials dealing with the siege are available in the large libraries in this country, such as the Library of Congress and the New York City Public Library, and, of course, in the libraries of Paris. However, of special importance is the splendid and complete Comte Alfred Boulay de la Meurthe collection of siege newspapers and periodicals now located in the Houghton Library of Harvard University. That library also contains the valuable Archibald Cary Coolidge collection of cartoons, *affiches,* pamphlets, and miscellaneous materials dealing with the siege. Both these collections have been of great value in this study.

This book is the outgrowth of a thesis presented for the Doctor of Philosophy degree at Harvard University, work

Preface

on which was made possible through fellowships provided by Amherst College and Harvard University. Thanks are owed to Professors Laurence B. Packard, E. Dwight Salmon, Alfred F. Havighurst, Charles L. Sherman, and President Charles W. Cole of Amherst College who first kindled my interest in history. Professors Crane Brinton, Sidney B. Fay, and Edward W. Fox, who read the original thesis, provided me with valuable suggestions which have found their way into this present book, as did Miss Lois Dwight Cole. My colleague, Professor Charles L. Sherman, has helped me in the arduous chore of proofreading, and my wife has aided in preparing the Index. Professor George B. Funnell has advised me on matters of French usage. In addition, I have received generous assistance in the preparation of this work from my family and the Trustees of Amherst College.

I am grateful also for the co-operation of the librarians of the following institutions: the Widener Library of Harvard University, the Houghton Library of Harvard University, the Library of Congress, the New York City Public Library, the Bibliothèque Nationale, and the Sorbonne.

Most of all, a great debt of gratitude is owed to Professor Donald Cope McKay of Harvard University, who has directed my interest in modern French history and continually guided my work. Naturally, I alone am responsible for the opinions and conclusions presented herein.

MELVIN KRANZBERG

Amherst College
August, 1949

ix

Contents

THE SIEGE OF PARIS, 1870–1871

Chapter 1

The Siege Is Set

Il ne faut pas qu'on s'ennuie—"Do not be bored"—
was the prime advice of Napoleon III's Imperial regime.
For eighteen years, enjoying the order and security which
the Second Empire gave it—and perhaps also as a reaction
against the "boredom" of Louis Philippe's July Monarchy—
Paris played. The court led the way by the example of its
lavish receptions and entertainments, and the rest of society
followed suit. Dull fetes and balls were the order of the
day for the materialistic and ostentatious Parisians whose
only aim was to make enough money so they could enjoy
themselves. The money-madness took the form of specula-
tion and gambling—millionaires were made overnight—
and it mattered not how one made his money, just so long
as he had it. In this atmosphere Paris became the cosmopolitan center of the universe; the Exposition of 1867 gave
proof of that by the list of foreign monarchs who visited
Paris at that time as well as by the number of foreigners who
came to the French capital to squander their fortunes on
wine, women, and song in the general recrudescence of
eighteenth-century morality.

In the midst of this gay, empty-headed life there was heard
a somber note—War! True, some farsighted observers had

1

suspected that Prussia's victory at Sadowa in 1866 marked a defeat for France as well as for Austria and had predicted that Napoleon III was leading France to destruction. But such harbingers of evil tidings were looked upon as rank pessimists or disaffected republicans who should have held their tongues when the Imperial edifice was covered with a façade of false liberalism. Even the declaration of war against Prussia on July 19, 1870—an act into which Bismarck had cunningly maneuvered the French government —could not disturb the Parisians in their mode of life. Was not Paris the capital of France, and was not France the greatest country of Europe?

Although some enemies of the regime were so unkind as to suggest that it was necessary for the Imperial secret police to organize "spontaneous" demonstrations for the war, there can be no doubt that Paris went to war with enthusiasm and with little foreboding for the future. The war was merely to be a glorious parade to Berlin, and the upstart Prussians would then very easily be put in their place. After having suppressed the *Marseillaise* for eighteen years, the Empire again allowed it to be sung in public, and its rousing strains contributed further to the martial ardor. Ollivier, the Prime Minister, was only expressing the sentiments of nearly everyone when he said, "It is with a light heart that the government of the Emperor sees war come." Actually, he meant that the government felt that the war had been forced upon it by the Prussians, and hence the Imperial regime bore no responsibility for the war guilt. But his ill-chosen words could also be interpreted to mean that the government viewed the serious matter of a war with Bismarck's coalition of German states lightly, and there can be no doubt that the majority of the French people believed that the war could be won without too much difficulty.

The Siege Is Set

As a matter of fact, the military record of the Second Empire looked good—on paper. Victories in the Crimean War and in the war with Austria, as well as successful colonial ventures in North Africa and Indo-China, prepared the French to believe that theirs was the best army in Europe. Besides, was not the Emperor the bearer of that awe-inspiring name—Napoleon? The Napoleonic legend helped make the French feel that defeat was impossible and that the war was going to be a gay, triumphant march to Berlin. The Germans were looked upon with contempt and scorn. They were thought to be weak in organization and intelligence and lacking in creative ability. While the Germans were being thus traduced, even by such a great historian as Michelet, as well as by a host of lesser literary lights, the French thought their own army to be the best equipped and trained in the world, their soldiers the most courageous, and their generals the best leaders. So great was their confidence in the success of their arms that the Parisians vied in making predictions—and even wagers—as to when and where victories would be won and peace signed. Officers were presented with ceremonial swords in order to be prepared for the triumphal entry into Berlin.

Unfortunately, the war was not to be won so easily. Despite the fact that the French possessed superior infantry arms, such as the *chassepot* and the *mitrailleuse,* ancestor of the modern machine gun, they were hopelessly outclassed by the superior Prussian artillery and generalship. The deciding factor was the pathetic inefficiency of the French preparations for supplies and mobilization. Although the Minister for War had assured his colleagues that the French army was ready "to the last button," the actual outbreak of the war revealed frightful disorder and extreme disorganization. It is no wonder that instead of the confidently awaited news of victory, there came reports of defeats at

Worth, Weissenburg, Mars-la-Tour, and Gravelotte, and of the shutting up of Bazaine's army in Metz.

Paris was stunned. How could the Empire, that solid regime of business and pleasure, be conquered so easily by the enemy whom it professed to scorn? Despite these defeats, the government still endeavored to deceive the public as to the immensity of the disasters. So great was the "will to believe" in eventual victory that Paris was half inclined to believe the Imperial propaganda. The city waited calmly for the news of a victory from MacMahon, sent out to relieve Bazaine; instead there came the news of the capitulation of the Emperor and the army at Sedan on September 2, 1870.

When the reports of the debacle at Sedan reached Paris on September 3, the ministers withheld it from the people, who nevertheless suspected that something was wrong from the number of rumors flying about. The following morning, Sunday, the government confirmed the news, and a general confusion arose. The populace gathered at the Corps Législatif on September 4, invaded it, and forced the proclamation of a Provisional Government, which, in accordance with accepted revolutionary procedure, proclaimed the Republic at the Hôtel de Ville, the City Hall of Paris.

The fall of the Empire was accomplished without a struggle. When the motion for the overthrow of the Imperial government was brought before the Corps Législatif, only a few voices were raised against it. And these voices did not attempt to defend the record of the Empire, but merely to question the legal right of the legislative body to vote the downfall of the government which had brought it into being. The hollowness of the political structure which Louis Napoleon had built was thus revealed in the ease with which it fell, although it must be said that even a government rooted more strongly in the affections of the people would have found it difficult to stand up under the impact of such a crushing military defeat. Despite Napoleon III's attempt to give his government more popular support by liberalizing it in its later years, the easy downfall of the Empire showed that it remained as it had been in the beginning—essentially the reign of an individual opportunist. Without the Emperor there could be no Empire.

The Corps Législatif, which contained a majority of Bonapartists, made no effective effort in behalf of the regime, and the mob did not even deign to invade the Senate, the other half of the legislative branch of the government. The senators waited hopefully for the uprising of September 4 to reach them and provide them with an excuse for doing nothing in behalf of the regime which had honored and enriched them, but the mob knew that the Senate commanded neither power nor popular support and ignored these impotent protégés of the Imperial regime. Invading the Corps Législatif and taking the republican leaders with them, the mob marched to the Hôtel de Ville, the traditional seat of revolutionary governments in Paris, while the Republic was proclaimed. The downfall of the Empire was not brought about by any one man or group of plotters. It came about "inevitably and invincibly" as the result of the impact of the news of a great disaster—succeeding many others —on a weak government which had forfeited all right to public sympathy and support—indeed, if it had ever had any such right.

As the Empress Eugénie slipped away from the palace to take refuge with the American Dr. Evans, and thence to travel to England, the mob invaded the Tuileries. It was extraordinarily well behaved and did not damage the "national property." The populace seemed happy with the overthrow of the Imperial government, and September 4 was a day of rejoicing rather than of bloodshed. Forgotten for a moment was the stupendous military defeat which jeopardized the safety of their city, while everyone rejoiced in the destruction of the despotism which had been stifling France for almost twenty years. In its happiness at being delivered from the "tyrant," Paris forgot the approaching enemy and abandoned itself to joy.

The men who achieved power on September 4—or, rather, those who suddenly found power thrust upon them —had formed part of the opposition under the Empire. Publicists, politicians, lawyers, and teachers for the most part, they had opposed Louis Napoleon's *coup d'état,* which had established him in power in 1851, and were, generally speaking, the leaders of the opposition. Now they were called upon to carry on a war which was not of their making. Perhaps that is what accounts for the composition of the stop-gap government that was set up. It gave itself the title of Government of National Defense, and only a coalition called into being by the exigencies of the military situation could have included so many disparate elements. Nearly every shade of political opinion was included within this hastily made up government except the by now thoroughly discredited Bonapartists. Indeed, almost the only thing which the members of the government had in common was their previous opposition to the Empire, and the fact that they comprised the Paris deputation in the Corps Législatif, that is, either men representing a Parisian constituency or who had been elected in Paris but who had opted for a constituency elsewhere under the system of allowing a man to run for office in several places at once.

Amid the tumult of September 4, the Republic had been proclaimed, and there were some active and open republicans to be found in the ranks of the government. In addition to men such as Arago and Gambetta, who had hastened to claim the Ministry of the Interior in order to keep it out of the hands of the more conservative Picard, there was the demagogic Rochefort. This darling of the populace had made his reputation by his scurrilous journalistic rantings against the Bonapartist regime, and his political opposition had won him a place in Napoleon III's well-filled jails. Liberated by the mob on September 4— physically but not spiritually chastened by his prison ordeal —Rochefort was added to the government because, as Jules Favre said, "It is better to have him with us than against us."

Despite the presence of these and other republicans within the government, the actual power was wielded by Legitimists, Orleanists, or other men of conservative stamp who did not wholly approve of the Republic whose defense they were now undertaking. Most important in this respect is General Trochu, who was made the president of the Government of National Defense, the most powerful and impressive post in the new administration. Trochu, Orleanist in sympathy, had been Military Governor of Paris. In that capacity he had promised the Empress that he would defend her and the regime, assuring her that she could rely upon his word as a "Catholic, Breton, and soldier." He had not been called upon to keep that promise. Now he was called upon to defend a city which he believed impossible of defense and to head a government in whose principles he did not believe. In that capacity, he showed himself to be only Catholic and Breton.

But subtle political distinctions were ignored by a populace undergoing a tremendous rebirth of enthusiasm after the downfall of the Empire. The original optimism with which they had gone to war had been tempered by the early defeats, but now these could be explained away by ascribing them to treason on the part of the deceased and unlamented Empire. Frenchmen could not believe that their armies had been defeated in a fair battle, and the cry of "treason" arose to explain the French losses. Everything was laid at the door of Napoleon and his government. Not content with blaming the Emperor for starting the war and making the defeats inevitable by the inefficiency of his military machine, the French accused the Empire of having destroyed their morale and character during its two decades of despotism.

All this was changed with the advent of the Republic, which, to many people, represented a magic formula which could chase demons and calm tempests. It was thought that victory would return to the French flag from the moment when it would no longer be dominated by the Imperial eagle. Jena, Austerlitz, Sebastopol, Magenta were forgotten; the eagle now symbolized Waterloo, Sedan. So much confidence was engendered by the change to the Republic that earnest republicans saw in the aurora borealis which lighted the sky the symbol of "the dawn of the victorious Republic," while others thought that the mere mention of the name "Republic" would terrify the Germans and change the complexion of affairs.

Faith in the Republic meant that the Parisians would devote themselves to its cause. Indeed, Paris showed itself more enthusiastic about the government which it had imposed upon France than did the rural areas, and the Parisians were almost frantic in manifesting their regard for the new government in the period immediately succeeding its birth. Furthermore, moralists who were perhaps better politicians than philosophers believed that a moral regeneration and a great reawakening of national consciousness would be brought about by the sufferings occasioned by the war and by the change in regimes. Robespierre's "Republic of Virtue" was going to be achieved on the third try!

Primarily responsible for the great faith in the reincarnated Republic was the myth of the great French Revolution. The very name "Republic" conjured up visions of that

First Republic of 1792 and 1793 which had hurled the enemies of France back from her borders. It was thought that
the new Republic, as its namesake, could "decree victory"
and, with the aid of the *levée en masse,* repulse the Prussians.
Only a few perspicacious observers saw the difference between myth and actuality and realized how much the Republic of 1870 differed from its greater namesake. Missing
was the "audacity" of which Danton had spoken almost a
century before; lacking also was the core of an army which
the Revolutionary generals had possessed. And von Moltke's
troops were far different from the mercenaries of the Duke
of Brunswick. But the Parisian "will to believe" in victory
brushed aside these practical objections to overconfidence.
The Republic had conquered once; it would conquer again.

Another myth shares some of the responsibility for making the Parisians believe in their invincibility; this was the
legend of the city of Paris. Parisians believed that their beloved city was the capital of "light and civilization" as well
as of France, and they credited their foes with the same love
and reverence for the city which they themselves felt. They
could not understand how the "barbarians" would dare
come against it. The incurable vanity at the bottom of the
Parisian disposition made it seem impossible to them that
anyone should bombard Paris; that would have been sacri-
legious. Victor Hugo was merely translating the sentiments
of his fellow Parisians when he gave eloquent expression
to the myth of Paris in an appeal to the Germans written
shortly after his return following the September revolution:

It is in Paris that the beating of Europe's heart is felt. Paris is
the city of cities. Paris is the city of men. There has been an
Athens, there has been a Rome, and there is a Paris. . . .

Is the nineteenth century to witness this frightful prodigy? A
nation fallen from polity to barbarism, abolishing the city of
nations; Germany extinguishing Paris; Germania lifting the axe

against Gaul! . . . Can you give this spectacle to the world? Can you, Germans, become Vandals again; personify barbarism decapitating civilization? . . .

Paris, pushed to extremities; Paris supported by all France aroused, can conquer and will conquer; and you will have tried in vain this course of action which already revolts the world.[1]

The welcome to the new regime made itself felt not only in expressions of jubilation and hope, but also in reaction to what had gone before. It was not enough to exalt the new regime; the old regime must be blackened. So, side by side with the enthusiastic reception given to the Republic, there came the "equal and opposite reaction" to the Empire and the effort to obliterate all reminders and remainders of the Napoleonic regime. The Imperial eagles, so much in evidence for the preceding two decades, were torn down from the public buildings to be replaced by the magic formula of "Liberty, Equality, Fraternity." At the Comédie Française, for example, the bust of Napoleon III was replaced by a bronze bust of *La République* which some foresighted and thrifty individual had preserved since 1848. A commission was appointed with the sole duty of renaming streets whose names were connected with the Empire. Thus the street called Dix-Decembre was changed to Quatre-Septembre; the avenue named after the Empress was now given the name of General Uhrich, the heroic defender of Strasbourg against the Prussian forces; and the Place Royal retook its denomination of the Place des Vosges. Indeed, some enterprising historian may yet write a history of France using as his chief source material the changes made in the names of streets in response to changes in regimes.

In addition to these outward and visible symbols of the inward and invisible grace conferred upon the Parisians

[1] Translation by Felix M. Whitehurst in *My Private Diary during the Siege of Paris* (London, 1875), I, 52–58.

by the conversion from Empire to Republic, there was an attempt made to oust all Imperial office holders and replace them with good republicans. This was not always accompanied with fortunate results, for many important offices were immediately invaded by ambitious and inexperienced new men who clogged the government machinery at a time when the need for quick action was paramount. But since it can hardly be said that the Imperial bureaucracy had distinguished itself by its efficiency in carrying on the war heretofore, perhaps the loss was not so great as the testimony of the disgruntled ex-officials would have us believe.

Every attempt was made to vilify the former government. Scandalous and obscene caricatures of Empress Eugénie were hawked in the streets, while Napoleon was accused of conspiring with Bismarck for the return of his dynasty to the throne in exchange for delivering France over to the Prussians. The ill-fated Emperor was nearly always derisively referred to as "Badinguet," the name of the workman in whose clothes Napoleon had escaped from the fortress of Ham in 1846, where he had been imprisoned for an attempt to overthrow the monarchy of Louis Philippe and institute an Imperial restoration. Napoleon's large nose gave the caricaturists the opportunity to paint a most unflattering picture of him, while the pious and staid Eugénie was depicted as a wanton, appearing in the scurrilous cartoons in the nude, being fondled by several men including a priest.

Badly written and printed libelous and scandalous brochures appeared on the streets almost overnight. The titles speak for themselves: *The Wife of Bonaparte—Her Loves, Her Orgies; Letters of Napoleon III to Marguerite Bellanger* (one of Louis' better-known mistresses); and many others. This insulting and gross literature aroused some Parisians of refinement and delicacy of taste to protest, but the new government, busy with other matters and containing men such as Rochefort, who had not hesitated to vilify the Imperial family even when it was still in power, was not minded to take energetic action against these attempts to smear its old enemy.

Indeed, the government itself was not above lending a hand in the matter of discrediting its predecessor. Shortly after its accession to power the government began the publication of the secret papers found in the Tuileries Palace under the title of *Papers and Correspondence of the Imperial Family*. Naturally, only the most colorful and spicy items were published, and these revealed a great deal of scandal and caused much talk. Certain astonishing facts came out, particularly in regard to the civil list, which showed that the government of the Empire had provided liberal pensions to many outsiders in addition to "the sisters and cousins and aunts" normally to be expected on such a list.

But the animus against the deceased Imperial government was mild compared to the virulent bitterness exhibited against the Prussians. After all, the Empire was dead; the Prussian threat remained, and, unlike the Irish, the Parisians thought in terms of the present danger rather than engaging constantly in battle against yesterday's foes. So, as time passed, the Empire was more or less forgotten, but hatred of the Germans continued. No name was too mean to be given them, and no feeling was too base to be attributed to them.

History was called upon to endorse this sentiment of enmity and, of course, came nobly forward to do the work of outraged nationalism. Typical of this was the journalistic study of the Prussian hero Blücher, who had played a part in defeating the first Napoleon at Waterloo. While granting that Blücher possessed certain military qualities of audacity, bravery, and tenacity, the study also pointed out that he was a typical Prussian hero in that he was a "braggart, haughty, brutal, and, this goes without saying, avid and rapacious." [2]

King William of Prussia, in a few months to be crowned Emperor William I of Germany, was represented as a throwback to the feudalism and savagery of the Middle Ages. Inasmuch as William was reputed to have said that he made war against Napoleon, not against France, the Parisians considered the future Kaiser to be personally responsible for the continuance of the war after the overthrow of the Empire. Even neutral opinion believed this to be a war of princes, not of peoples, and the American statesman Charles Sumner was surprised that the war continued after the capture of one of the princely protagonists. Mr. Sumner can hardly be condemned at this late date for his naïveté on this point, especially since, after eighty years and two World Wars, American politicians still find it difficult to understand the bitter national differences and feelings which animate and explain many of Europe's actions. At any rate, the Parisians of 1870 found it an easy matter to concentrate their Prussophobia on the person of the Prussian king. Such was the feeling against him that a subscription was started in Paris for a musket of honor to be given to the man who shot the ruler of Prussia, the musket to bear the inscription "Peacemaker." Evidently the subscribers did not stop to consider that if the war had not ceased when Napoleon had been erased from the picture, it would be hardly likely to make much difference if William were also disposed of.

Indicative of the venom displayed toward the Prussians was the number of atrocity stories which found willing listeners. The following story, taken from a Paris news-

[2] *Le Moniteur Universel,* Nov. 23, 1870.

paper of September 12, 1870, is typical of those believed by an all too credulous audience:

> In the church of Bazeilles, eighty people, mostly women and children, were burned alive, deliberately. These people were all unarmed and had believed that the sanctity of the place would protect them from the ferocity of the barbarians: not only was their hope deceived, but this horrible massacre took place in full daylight, and officers assisted in it; soldiers placed at the exits used their bayonets to prevent escape.[3]

No mention of this particular act can be found in any other records, and the same might also be said of many of the accusations of rape and deliberate shelling of hospitals which were leveled at the Prussians. But these atrocity stories were so popular that the sensational press found it profitable to cater to the demand, and one newspaper carried a feature column entitled "Prussian Savagery," which appeared regularly throughout the siege. Nor were the other newspaper editors lacking in the type of lurid imagination necessary to engage in this competition of atrocity propaganda. Officialdom encouraged, or at least did nothing to prevent, the circulation of such stories, and the diplomatic agents of France were directed to protest to the outside world against Prussian brutality in carrying on the war.

The French could not, or would not, believe that they were being beaten fairly and squarely by the Prussians. Their defeats were attributed in great part to Prussian espionage and the existence of a German spy ring in France before the war. The great historian Michelet complained, "Using the magnifying-glasses given by passion, hatred, envy, and fanaticism, the young devout missionaries of Teutonic mania came among us, to examine everything

---

[3] *Le Peuple Français,* Sept. 12, 1870.

and send home accurate statistics about everything." This unconscious tribute to the thoroughness of the German preparations was echoed, although with somewhat less basis, by the cautious Goncourt, who reported in his journal: "While going down the Champs-Elysées, I look at the closed house of Paiva [great star of the Paris stage under the Empire], and I wonder if this has not been a great bureau of Prussian espionage in Paris."

Belief in Prussian adeptness in trickery and espionage was so widely held that any news which was unfavorable to the French was suspected to be a Prussian ruse which was not to be credited. So perverted did the French sense of fair play become, through hatred of the Germans, that four captured Prussian officers allowed the freedom of the city were set upon by the Parisians. General Trochu, a soldier in at least this respect, reminded the populace that these officers, prisoners on parole, as were the captive French officers in Prussia, were placed under the safeguard of the "national honor." But this appeal to the "national honor" did not go unchallenged; hatred of Prussians, even those who had been so considerate of France as to surrender to French troops, was so great that commentators were not slow in pointing out that Trochu was comparing "two essentially different situations." Germany, thus far victorious in the war, could afford to be magnanimous to the captured enemy; whereas the French had no obligation to be generous to an enemy "who have spied on us for many years, and who have only one dream: our destruction."

The Parisians refused to credit their enemies with any virtues whatsoever. Even the scientific methods of warfare employed by the Prussians were looked upon as symptoms of cowardice, and they were said to have "substituted mathematics for courage." Michelet, the historian mindful of the personal nature of combat in the past, turned the impersonal nature of modern warfare into a criticism of the enemy, stating:

> This new art of killing a people at 5000 meters' range, without any personal risk, without being even aware of the terrible consequences of the fire; does it not involve an impassiveness, a ruthlessness, which could not belong to foreign wars? It is, to say the least, cold-blooded murder. . . . [Frenchmen] would have felt disgraced to attack an enemy, as is done now, after having battered him with a storm of shells.[4]

No one ventured to remind Michelet that the French had prided themselves on the *chassepot* and *mitrailleuse,* potent scientific agents of destruction themselves, at the beginning of the war. And even though no one doubted that one Frenchman was equal to at least three Prussians in combat, it was still felt that there was something essentially dishonorable in the Prussians having superiority in numbers over the French troops!

Men of learning stepped forward to give a philosophical and scholarly basis to the hatred of Prussia. Members of the learned societies deplored the fact that Germany had departed from the teachings of Kant in "this scholarly and savage war which unites the precision of the mathematician to the stupid joy of the Vandal." Attempts were made to penetrate into the reasons for the behavior of the Germans who dared attack the French "apostles of peace." While endeavoring to retain scholarly calm and philosophical aloofness, the moralists and philosophers somehow managed to arrive at a view of the Prussians which did not differ a great deal in its hatred from that possessed by the less scholarly mass of the people. The difference between the thoughts of the scholars and the popular dislike of the

---

4 Jules Michelet, *France before Europe* (Boston, 1871), pp. 44–45.

Prussians was not one of degree or kind; it was merely stated in somewhat more grammatical—but perhaps less clear—language. Ivory towers no longer provided an effective defense against the shellbursts of prejudice and hatred which accompanied modern nationalist warfare. In brief, philosophy became highbrow propaganda.

Religion did not lag behind its philosophical ally in its concern for France. The Archbishop of Paris indicated, in a pastoral letter, that the Church must stand behind the national effort to free the country from the German invader and that "our duties towards God must not make us forget our duties towards France." Although the Church made no official pronouncement, many devout Catholics probably felt that the war partook of a crusade against Protestantism, represented by Prussia. They were prepared to fight the old type of religious warfare. The majority of Frenchmen, however, had no such need of secondary considerations; they were fighting the new type of religious warfare, that involving rival nationalisms.

The religion of nationalism, despite its warlike manifestations, also involved a set of ethical and moral attitudes not unlike those of the more traditional religions. This was especially the case because French nationalism, after September 4, again became the handmaid of republicanism, which, as during the 1790's, sought expression in a Republic of Virtue. The puritanical tenor of the various revolutionary governments in France has always made them think of the regeneration of national life in terms larger than those of civic virtue and public morality; the Republic of Virtue of Robespierre extended its domain into the realm of private morality and individual virtue. So did the Republic of 1870.

This was made easier by the memory of the loose morals and dissipation of social life under the Imperial regime.

The staunch republicans of 1870 believed that September 4 had overthrown not only an administrative system but had also accomplished a revolution in morals. Virtue and humanity were associated with a republic, and overnight France was to be purged of all social evils. Surprisingly enough, the new Republic did succeed in establishing some measure of virtue when it came to certain types of crime, but it is doubtful if any of the more common human vices were affected by the change in government. The downfall of the Empire had as an immediate consequence a short period of disorder and lawlessness, but the growth in the organization of the Government of National Defense soon brought order out of the confusion. One of the first measures undertaken by the new regime was a gigantic "dragnet" to purge Paris of the refugees from justice, gamblers, cheats, pimps, prostitutes, and other undesirable persons who abounded in the cosmopolitan capital. The city became relatively free from crime in the sense of murder, robbery, theft, and street brawls. But whether this was due to a moral regeneration brought about by the birth of the new Republic or simply to the constant presence of armed patrols of soldiers on the streets every night is a question which the republican chroniclers of the siege have never bothered to face.

But the most pressing problem facing the new government was not that of crime, nor even the liquidation of the old regime and the installation of the new, but that of national defense. The defeat at Sedan did not mean the end of the war; it merely meant the closing of one phase of the campaign and the opening of another. The German armies were descending on Paris, and it was necessary that the government improvise some defense at once, if it were decided that Paris was to be defended.

If this had been purely a military question, then it is

probable that the decision would have been against defending Paris, for the military leaders were agreed that defense was useless and victory impossible. But, as one officer stated, "Whatever way one envisaged the value of the elements of resistance which remained in France, or even admitting the impossibility of victory under our flag, one thing was certain: our honor is engaged not to permit the Germans to enter Paris without striking a blow." [5] The military leaders were willing to abandon sound military reasoning and to attempt a defense in whose success they had no confidence.

The political leaders, especially those of republican persuasion, did not bother themselves with the quest for that elusive entity known as "honor." Fortified with the myth of the power of the name of the Republic and of Paris, they believed that ultimate victory could be achieved. The tacit defeatism that marked the attitude of the military was not shared by the politicians of republican stamp. Political and emotional considerations thus prevailed over a careful estimate of the military situation, and it was decided that the government was to stay in the capital and attempt to defeat the Prussians from there. Yet this government which pledged itself to victory was headed by one of those same military men, Trochu, who did not believe in the efficacy of the defense which he now found himself obliged to conduct and who was certain of its ultimate failure. Indeed, it might not be too venturesome to suggest that he would have welcomed such a failure, for Trochu was a pious Breton with Orleanist sympathies. He did not believe in a republic, although he had persuaded his colleague in the government, Jules Ferry, that he was determined to carry out a successful defense of the Republic and its capital, while at the same time asserting

---

[5] Arthur Ballue, *Les Zouaves à Paris pendant le siège* (Paris, 1872), p. 16.

to his military staff that resistance was nothing more than a "heroic folly."

But this defeatism of the generals was not manifested in the period from September 4 to the time when Paris was completely invested on September 19. Then the emphasis was on a serious attempt to prepare the city for military events, while the government also sought to strengthen itself politically. On September 6, Jules Favre, Vice-President of the Republic and Minister of Foreign Affairs, issued his famous circular to France's diplomatic representatives in which he declared that France would not give up "an inch of her territory nor a stone of her fortresses." Experts after the event have criticized Favre for this statement which, they said, made negotiations for peace under favorable circumstances virtually impossible, but it is hard to see how an official of a government which had in its title the words "National Defense" could have acted otherwise. Besides, the Parisians still believed victory possible, and it would have been political suicide for the new administration to have started out with an announcement that it was willing to give up territory to an enemy which it believed had not yet won the war. In the light of subsequent events, Favre's statement may appear to have been mere braggadocio, but on September 6, 1870, it revealed the temper of the French people as perhaps no other statement could have done.

That the new regime was a true coalition government comprising all political elements (except the thoroughly discredited Bonapartists) was revealed by the employment of Thiers, the old minister of Louis Philippe who had headed the moderate opposition to the Empire. Thiers was sent on a diplomatic mission to England, Austria, and Russia in an attempt to enlist outside aid in behalf of France. However, Bismarck's diplomatic preparations had been so thorough that the best the aged French politician could obtain was a sympathetic hearing, owing perhaps more to his own personality than to the cause which he represented. The monarchs of Europe had not forgotten the threat of the First French Republic, and even in England approbation was moderate. Only in America, which Thiers did not visit, was there any genuine enthusiasm shown for the new French government, but the United States did not yet feel itself affluent enough to repay the debt to Lafayette at this time. The mission of Thiers was doomed to failure, although he did succeed in laying the French case before the world.

Realizing that Paris might be completely cut off from the rest of France as well as the rest of the world in case the city were completely invested, the government decided to send a delegation to the French provinces as well as to the foreign courts of Europe. Thus, a delegation was sent to Tours in order to govern the rest of France, while the central government remained in Paris.

In addition to these diplomatic and political maneuvers, the Government of National Defense made frantic efforts to prepare the city militarily. Manpower was needed as well as fortifications. The Provincial Mobile Guard was called in to defend the capital, with General Vinoy's forces, which had advanced too slowly to be captured at Sedan. The rolling stock of the Northern and other railroads was sent to the east to bring back other troops from the front. In addition to the regular troops brought into Paris, the National Guard was also called upon to furnish the soldiers necessary to defend the city. This military institution had been in existence for many years, but the Empire had limited its numbers and had carefully chosen its members from a restricted group of "safe" bourgeoisie. Under the pressure of the war with Prussia, the Empress, acting as regent in Paris, had authorized the reorganization of the Guard and enrollment in its ranks on a more democratic basis on August 12, 1870. This reorganization accomplished little, but the new government decreed on September 6 the organization of sixty new battalions. The response to this was greater than had been anticipated. Instead of sixty new units being formed, enough men responded to make 194 battalions, and the National Guard overnight grew in number from 90,000 to more than 300,000 potential fighting men. Patriotism rather than economic materialism was undoubtedly the motive for this overwhelming response, for it was not until a week later that the government decided to vote pay for service in the National Guard.

The democratization of the National Guard was furthered by a decree of September 16 which discharged the officers of the Guard who had been Imperial appointees and provided for election of officers by the troops themselves; this was to be a democratic army if not a fighting army. Control of the National Guard was not vested in the Ministry of War, as might be expected, but in the Ministry of Interior, indicating that their duties might be more along policing lines than as combat troops on the fighting front. But at least the new Republic had called into being a fighting force composed of almost all the able-bodied men of Paris which might prove to be of valuable assistance in the struggle with the hated Prussians.

Meanwhile, the outlying forts in the vicinity of Paris were abandoned because it would have required too much work and time to get them in readiness, and it was decided that the defense was to be made in the immediate environs of the city. Houses in a "military zone" established by the government were abandoned or demolished, and the suburban dwellers streamed into Paris, leaving their homes vacant and the streets of the suburbs deserted. Only some insulting inscriptions chalked on the walls, such as "Death to the Prussians" or "Two heads worth three cents—William and Bismarck," gave evidence that the Germans were soon expected. A decree of September 10 ordered that all forests and woods which might hamper the defense of Paris by giving shelter to the Prussians and screening their troop movements were to be burned down, and the forests of Montmorency and Bundy were thus treated, as well as portions of the woods of Boulogne and Vincennes.

Exterior works and breastworks were constructed near the forts; barracks and powder magazines were armor-plated; quarries were filled up; houses which might aid the enemy attack were demolished; and bridges were undermined. A beginning was also made in digging entrenchments connecting the forts.

Within the city proper, a committee headed by Rochefort was appointed to attend to the building of ramparts and barricades, in case the Prussians should attempt to take the city by assault and it should come to hand-to-hand combat. The work of this committee went for nought, so far as providing military protection against the Prussians, but these barricades were to be useful a few months later when Parisians used them against one another in the Commune.

Military preparations included a great deal besides the actual defensive works. Barracks, hospitals, and factories dotted the city. The newly completed Opera House was transformed into a military and provision depot, and there was constant signaling from its roof to other semaphore stations atop the Arc de Triomphe, the Pantheon, the Ministry of Marine, the heights of Montmartre, and the great fort of Mont Valérien. At night electric searchlights were used for signaling purposes, an innovation for that time.

Railway workshops became cannon foundries, and tobacco factories became arsenals. Pictures were removed from the great gallery of the Louvre, and it became transformed into a vast armament shop. Balloons were manufactured at the Orleans station, while the Lyons railroad depot made cannon, and the North railway station had mills set up for grinding flour. A uniform factory was established in the Gaîté theater, and hospitals were to be found everywhere—in hotels, department stores, theaters, and public buildings. Thus the flag of the Red Cross waved from such varied buildings as the Odéon, Comédie-Française, Variétés, Lyrique, Port St. Martin, Cluny, and Belleville theaters, and from the Tuileries, Luxembourg, Elysées, Palais Royal, Corps Législatif, Palais de Justice, and the Café de la Cascade.

Paris was filled with military camps. The Tuileries gardens became an artillery bivouac, and the Napoleon and Empress Circuses were transformed into barracks for the Mobile Guard coming into the city. Constant marching and drilling went on throughout the city and made it appear to be a gigantic military establishment, as indeed it was rapidly becoming. The Bois de Boulogne was a park for animals, actually a tremendous stockyard. Its trees were later destroyed for fuel, as were those of the Bois de Vincennes and those on the Champs Elysées and the avenues Montaigne and Bugeaud.

Indeed, all business was profoundly changed by the exigencies of the military situation. "Business as usual" could not be the order of the day, and the character of the business that remained changed from one dealing with articles of peace to one concentrated on articles of war. Guns, kepis, and plastrons replaced the luxury trades as the sinews of business in Paris, and the inventive facilities of the city were concentrated on the problem of the readiest means of taking human life. As the Prussian armies swooped down on Paris and cut it off from the outside world, the wholesale exporting houses closed of necessity. But most of the retail stores kept open as usual. Jewelers, modistes, and department stores remained open, but they did little business, since they had only their old stock to sell and many people were too preoccupied with military affairs to buy. As might be expected, the grocers, butchers, and markets prospered as everyone hastened to lay in a supply of food and thus be protected from shortages created by his neighbor's hoarding.

Industry boomed during the siege, many factories being converted in order to manufacture war materials. Although there were occasional debates as to whether private industry should be allowed to make some guns of a new breech-loading model, it was necessary to turn to private industry for the production of armaments, and all sorts of experts, under the leadership of a Committee of Civil Engineering, took over the administration of the work. Indeed, there was very little else for private industry to do but manufacture war materials, since there was practically no demand for its ordinary products. No private building was being carried on, so masons and carpenters could ply their craft only on "work for the defense." There was no market for the luxurious creations of the Paris *couturiers*, so the unemployed seamstresses took jobs manufacturing cartridges at the tobacco factories which had been converted to that purpose.

Thanks to various measures, the financial situation in Paris did not raise any considerable embarrassment. By a series of decrees payment of rent and bills of exchange was deferred, so that it required little ready money to live from day to day. Financially, transactions at the Bourse were trifling, although customers stood around and tried to emulate the din of more peaceful days by shouting out the prices for stocks for which there were no buyers. The staff officers of the 181st Battalion of the National Guard were established within the Bourse building, but that did not prevent the dyed-in-the-wool speculators from meeting one another beneath the colonnade and talking of stocks while dreaming of profits.

The transition to a stricter war economy could even be noticed in such unglamorous pursuits as the sanitary arrangements for the city. While assuring the Parisians that the change in regimes and the Prussian invasion would not affect the quality of the city's sanitation facilities, the Mayor, Arago, appointed a Central Commission of Health and Hygiene. It was generally charged with the cleansing of wells, the collection of rubbish, and the supervision of other health projects. Despite this Commission and the Mayor's assurances, it cannot be said the health provisions of the city did not suffer. The problem of sewage disposal, for example, was a serious one. This was the age of "outdoor plumbing," and the removal of waste was made difficult by the military operations in the vicinity of Paris. When the sewage could no longer be taken outside the city, *dépôts de fumier* were established at about twenty points in the peripheral arrondissements, so that the city was surrounded by a belt of sewage. In addition, the service of collecting this waste matter functioned imperfectly because the war had disrupted its personnel. This task was normally entrusted almost entirely to Germans, but these had left Paris at the outbreak of the war, and the loss of such a large percentage of the workers in this occupation rendered the service inefficient. In this one respect at least—the collection of sewage—the Parisians were willing to admit to German efficiency and superiority. As it was, the nose as well as the eyes of Paris could not fail to perceive the changes being wrought in the city as it prepared for a siege.

The change in the physical appearance of Paris, caused by the military preparations evoked by the coming siege, was also paralleled in the costumes of the people themselves. Military dress was prevalent everywhere, for everybody was, or tried to appear to be, a soldier. The hawkers on the street gave respect to their calling by wearing uniforms, and some individuals wore their National Guard uniforms while carrying on their daily nonmilitary business. Even those ineligible to wear a regular uniform wore some combination of "uniform" of their own design. So it was not considered strange to see a man dressed in half-civilian, half-military outfit, or to see epaulettes sewed on to regular suit jackets, or people in normal civilian clothes wearing swords, or ordinary pants with stripes sewed down them. Even the septuagenarian Victor Hugo, ineligible to belong to any military formation, could not resist the romantic appeal of military dress and always appeared in public wearing a kepi without insignia or numbers.

Women's fashions, of course, also responded quickly to the changed conditions. Crinoline had been the favorite dress of the early period of the Empire, and it had continually grown larger and more ornate. Suddenly, in 1867, the crinoline had gone out of style, its place being taken by the bustle and drapes. While the Empire was thinning out, Empress Eugénie, the fashion plate of the era, was spreading out, so that she looked better without frills and furbelows. As a result, the gowns gradually became straighter and less bulky as the ladies of fashion accommodated their own wardrobes to the increasing girth of the

Empress. Despite these changes, the coming of the war brought a transformation in the mood of women's dresses, even though it may not have accomplished the introduction of a completely "new look." The nurses' uniforms and the somber dresses of the women were in marked contrast to previous times. As one Frenchman plaintively observed, "No coquetry. . . . The Parisiennes . . . [appear] like nuns—sadly dressed, sadly nourished, and scarecrowish."

Despite the feverish preparations for a siege—sartorial, sanitary, and otherwise—the Parisians still did not seem to believe in the possibility of such a siege. They did not despair, for it seemed impossible to them that the "barbarians" would besiege the "city of light." The reports from the provinces and the official communiqués of the government that the Germans were marching on Paris apparently did not succeed in convincing many thousands of people in the capital who seriously maintained that the Germans would never dare invest their beloved city.

And was not Paris invincible? Even if the Germans really were coming, the journalists and armchair strategists had written a number of articles to demonstrate that Paris could never be invested by less than 1,500,000 men—1,200,000 at the very least—and that a place of war which could revictual itself and maintain free communications was impregnable. On the very eve of the siege, one newspaper did not hesitate to reassure its readers that any fears they might have because of the disaster of Sedan and the approach of the Prussian army were exaggerated. It was an easy matter for the journalists to prove that in every battle the enemy losses had been greater than those of the French, and to claim that dysentery was ravaging the Prussian army to such an extent that the tremendous loss sustained by the surrender at Sedan had been more than compensated, so that France had fewer men *hors de combat* than her adversaries. Furthermore, the potential besiegers of the capital were undoubtedly so fatigued by their march across France that they would be no match for the rested defenders of the fortresses of Paris. Finally, Paris being a fortified city, it would be necessary for the invaders to besiege one or two of the outlying forts at first, in which case they would be caught between the converging fires of the fortifications both in front and behind the attacked fortresses, and even the King of Prussia would hesitate to commit his soldiers—"no matter how cheaply he holds their lives"—to such mass slaughter. In fine, Paris could not be besieged, and, even if it were, France possessed "all the resources necessary to conquer the invaders and exterminate them." [6]

The optimistic view given above, to which many Frenchmen subscribed, was printed on September 17, the date on which Paris cut its last railroad lines to the outside. On the following day, the Prussian advance guards arrived before the city, and on September 19, after some fighting, the French troops evacuated the plateau of Châtillon, which the enemy promptly occupied, along with positions at Villejuif, Clamart, and Meudon. The investment of Paris by the armies of the Crown Prince of Prussia and Prince Albert of Saxony was now complete. Paris was completely cut off from the outside world by a ring of German troops.

---

[6] Quotations, direct and indirect, are from *La Guerre Illustré*, Sept. 17, 1870.

Chapter 11

The Siege Must Go On

The siege was no longer a vague possibility; it was now a reality. It was no longer enough merely to proclaim that Paris could not be invested, or that, if it could be besieged, the siege could not be carried through to a successful conclusion. It was now necessary that some genuine measures be taken to defend the city, for the last chance of avoiding, by diplomatic or military means, the encirclement of the capital had been unsuccessful. The evacuation of the plateau of Châtillon had meant that fighting could not prevent the full encirclement, and the failure of Jules Favre's peace negotiations with Bismarck had shown the futility of diplomatic negotiations in trying to prevent Paris from becoming a battleground.

Lord Granville, the English statesman, had arranged the interview between Favre, Vice-President of the Government of National Defense and its Foreign Minister, and Bismarck, in order to prevent further bloodshed. Had Bismarck's demands been fairly reasonable, the Government of National Defense, pledged to defeat the Prussians, might have accepted them, and this government, called into being at a time of crisis, would have gone down in history as a defense government which had made no efforts to defend anything. As it was, Bismarck believed the French to be thoroughly crushed already, and he demanded the cession of Alsace and Lorraine as well as immediate possession of strong points such as Metz, Strasbourg, and Mont Valérien, the fortress commanding Paris. The extent of Bismarck's demands succeeded in making the government perforce a Government of National Defense; it had to fight. Favre was willing to concede an indemnity to Prussia, reimbursing it for the "cost" of the war. He was prepared also to agree to the dismantling of Metz, Strasbourg, and other fortifications. But he had already pledged the French people that he would not yield "one inch of French territory." Despite Favre's tears, Bismarck was unmoved by an attitude which he described as one of "Take our gold, but leave our country." The cession of territory was as indispensable to him as it was inadmissible to the French. Bismarck's propositions were indignantly rejected when Favre returned on September 21 from Ferrières and reported the results of the negotiations. The government now had no other recourse than to defend the country.

September 21 also happened to be the seventy-eighth anniversary of the founding of the First French Republic, so while the government hastened to reject Bismarck's demands, the more republican elements within the administration, notably Gambetta and Arago, issued proclamations reminding the people of the glorious conduct of Frenchmen in 1792 and held that up as an example for France to follow in her present predicament. Victor Hugo also used this date as an occasion to issue one of his own private proclamations, apparently designed to whip the Parisians into a frenzy of resistance by means of rhetoric. These who wanted to believe in the future of France could not fail to be impressed by his words:

The Siege of Paris

The Prussians have decreed that France shall be Germany and Germany Prussia. That I, as a Lorrainer, am a German; that the Nile, the Tiber, and the Seine are affluents of the Sarre; that the city which for centuries has enlightened the globe is superfluous, Berlin henceforth being capable of settling all matters; that Montaigne, Rabelais, Pascal, Molière, Diderot, Rousseau, Danton, and the French Revolution never existed; that, having Bismarck, we do not need Voltaire, but the universe belongs to the conquered of Napoleon the Great and the conquerors of Napoleon the Little; that henceforth thought, conscience, poetry, art, will begin at Potsdam and finish at Spandau. . . . This, dearest Parisians, they are executing upon you. When they suppress Paris they mutilate the world; their attack is aimed *urbi et orbi*. Is such a future possible? We answer only by a smile. . . . Attack Paris, then; blockade, bombard her. Try it; but while you are about to unite, snow, sleet, hail, rain, frost, and ice will come. Paris will defend herself. Paris, which has been accustomed to amuse mankind, will now terrify it. The world will be amazed. . . .

But bombs—not bombast—are needed to win a war.

General Trochu, while not taken in by the militant enthusiasm of Victor Hugo or of the man in the street to whom the romantic poet addressed his exhortations, cautiously determined to try the strength of the forces he had at his disposal in the defense of the capital. He decided to embark upon a series of small sallies to test the mettle of his troops and see whether they could eventually be converted into a first-class fighting force, and, at the same time, to probe the Prussian circle and test its vulnerability. The first of these preliminary sorties was made during the night of September 22 and early morning of September 23 in the direction of the heights of Villejuif on the south of Paris, with no special advantage being gained.

Meanwhile Paris received some unwelcome news. Reports of the fall of Toul, which had been besieged since the middle of August, were received on September 26, and the great fortress of Strasbourg, with 10,000 beleaguered troops, surrendered on September 27. This latter was a great blow to the people of Paris, because the heroic defense of the Alsatian city by General Uhrich had excited the admiration of the Parisian populace, and the inevitable yet unexpected fall of the city might have given them pause to think of the future in store for their own besieged city. The admiration of Strasbourg's defense had assumed the proportions of a cult. The statue of the city in the Place de la Concorde had become a place of pilgrimage for patriotic Frenchmen, who decorated it with tricolors and flowers and made it the scene of innumerable popular "manifestations."

These "manifestations" and deputations to the government provided a harmless outlet to the patriotic energies of many Parisians. A typical "manifestation" of this sort usually consisted of marching to the statue of Strasbourg and laying wreaths at its base, singing the *Marseillaise,* listening to a fiery orator holding forth at the statue, and then parading to the square in front of the City Hall where the government met. After shouting "No peace!" a few times, the marchers would parade down the boulevards and disperse for their homes, satisfied that they had done their best and deserved well of their country. The attraction of the Statue of Strasbourg was in no sense diminished because a workman had seen fit to chip off its nose a few months before because, as he explained it, "It reminded me of my wife." The fall of Strasbourg increased the number of "manifestations" held in honor of the city because it was known that Bismarck had demanded its cession to Prussia, and the city was considered to be a martyr for

33

France. Indeed, it was not until the end of November that these parades and speeches before that statue diminished somewhat in intensity.

Not all the manifestations centered in the "cult" of Strasbourg. Demonstrations were organized for practically every purpose under the sun. They were publicized by posters and newspapers which convoked the National Guard, gave the time and place of the meeting, and explained the purpose of the manifestation. It was always thought desirable to have as many of the National Guard as possible at any such demonstration, for their presence with arms indicated the seriousness of the gathering and the patriotism of its motives. These demonstrations were not officially sponsored, and almost invariably they ended by marching to the City Hall where the government was forced to receive the delegations. Reception of the manifestants required so much of the government's time that soon various members were appointed to speak to them and thus to divide the labor. Some typical manifestations were as follows: September 21—a demonstration by the heads of the battalions of the National Guard against any armistice; September 22—a manifestation led by some fervent patriots asking for "energetic action," the *levée en masse,* erection of barricades, and the postponement of municipal elections; September 26—the mayors of Paris paraded to the government to demand a mass levy.

These demonstrations were small, but some of them were highly organized and included as many as 10,000 marchers. This was particularly the case of those organized by the radicals who were impatient at the supposed inaction of the government. The surrender of Toul and Strasbourg made some of them believe that the government had been remiss in not saving those cities from the Prussians. The Government of National Defense had not acted in the way the First Republic had done. Its record in averting defeat was so far no better than that of the Second Empire which it had replaced. Furthermore, Trochu's cautious policy did not appear to be achieving results satisfactory to these impatient Frenchmen. On September 30 he had launched a small sortie in the direction of Chevilly for the purpose of trying his unseasoned troops in the presence of the enemy and in an effort to find out the extent of the Prussian siege works. This sortie had succeeded in advancing beyond the German advance posts to the Prussian main line at Thiais and Choisy-le-Roi, where, after a strong assault which failed to shake the Prussian line, the defenders of Paris withdrew to their previous positions. These tactics did not appeal to the hotheaded patriots who could see no reason for withdrawal after having acquired some territory from the enemy.

Perhaps because of the impatience aroused by these cautious tactics, Admiral Fourichon resigned his portfolio in the War Ministry on October 3 but remained in the government as the head of the Navy, which played an important role during the siege by manning the large guns of the fortresses. But this resignation did not satisfy the radicals. On October 6, Citizen Flourens, one of the most popular and active radicals, headed a demonstration of 10,000 men who marched to the City Hall. Arriving at their destination, Citizen Flourens presented the demands of his group, composed chiefly of working-class patriots from the proletarian Belleville section, calling for more energetic pursuit of the defense of Paris. He demanded that the National Guard be armed with *chassepots* which were much more efficient than the old rifles which had been issued them. Flourens also demanded that "the Imperial system of opposing one Frenchman to three Prussians be abandoned," as if the Imperial regime and the Government of National Defense had consciously endeavored to put their troops at a numerical disadvantage whenever they faced the enemy. Of course, as throughout the siege, the demands of Flourens, as well as most radicals versed in the tradition of the French Revolution, included the *levée en masse*. Flourens also asked that Garibaldi, the fiery Italian national patriot and defender of liberty, be called to the aid of the French Republic, and that all "suspicious persons," i.e., nonrepublicans, be dismissed from the administration. After presentation of these demands to the government, Flourens led his 10,000 armed marchers back to Belleville, and the incident was apparently forgotten.

But the government did not accede to the demands of Flourens and his paraders, and on October 8 the clamor for a more energetic defense, based upon the traditional French Revolutionary lines involving a *levée en masse* and action by a resuscitated "Commune" of Paris, took the form of an abortive revolt fomented by Sapia, one of the more persistent radicals commanding a National Guard battalion from the Belleville section. But evidently Sapia's mistrust of the government's ability to conduct the defense of Paris was not shared by his men, for instead of acceding to his desire to march on the City Hall and force the government to pursue a more energetic policy, his men seized him and turned him over to his military superiors. Indeed, even the 5 battalions of the National Guard from Belleville who had marched in the demonstration led by Flourens a few days before wished to assure the government of their friendly feelings despite the rebuff of their demands. As a result, they invited Ferry to pass them in review, and this moderate member of the government reviewed them on October 11. The lone man who endeavored to cry out for the reorganization of the government along communal lines during this review was forcibly dealt with by his comrades.

The Siege Must Go On

One reason why these proletarian patriots of the National Guard were desirous of showing their friendliness toward the government was because at last it seemed ready to do something about the defense of France. Gambetta, the staunch and energetic republican who served as Minister of Interior, was dispatched to Tours in an effort to organize the Delegation which the government had previously sent there and to endeavor to rally all France's resources to the aid of its beleaguered capital. After the fall of Strasbourg and Toul, the government had realized that Paris was doomed unless help should be forthcoming from the outside. Stronger efforts must be made to organize resistance outside the capital if it were to be saved.

Considering the strategy which the Prussians were following, this was the proper move for the government to take. The failure of the Prussians to bombard Paris and to advance farther than the outlying districts made the Parisians realize that an attempt was to be made to starve them out while Prussian detachments leisurely mopped up the rest of France. French recruiting was at a standstill, and military organization outside of Paris had virtually ceased, although the Delegation to the provinces was endeavoring to remedy the situation. While French provincial cities were falling one by one, Paris would become weaker and weaker as the hope of outside support also faded away. Obviously something had to be done to provide an effective resistance in the provinces, and just as obviously this task had to be entrusted to Gambetta, one of the few men in the government who really believed that such resistance could be effective.

Gambetta's departure to Tours on October 7 was by means of balloon. With Paris completely blockaded by the Prussians, the air was the only free route for the communications necessary for carrying on a military campaign and governing the country. The siege of Paris was notable with respect to the communications problem, since it was the first attempt to resort to the air for communications on a large scale, and it was done fairly successfully.

September 19 was the date of the last regular mail delivery in Paris, and on September 21, Nadar, the aeronaut, made an experimental flight in a balloon to test its possibilities as a communications medium from the besieged city. M. Nadar used this opportunity to drop handbills over the Prussian lines, telling them of the horrors they were committing in besieging the center of civilization. These handbills were not, as some cynics alleged, advertisements of Nadar's own company. This flight proved that balloons could be used practicably for carrying information to the outside world, and on September 23 the "Neptune," an old balloon belonging to the Administration of War which had been used to stir up interest during public celebrations, left the city with 103 kilograms of letters to inaugurate the regular balloon service.

In the meantime, two factories were set up in Paris to manufacture new balloons, while Tissandier, another aeronaut, was sent to the provinces to organize communications there. The success of the balloon method can be seen from the fact that during the entire siege approximately sixty-five balloons were dispatched from Paris, carrying 2,500,000 letters weighing 10,000 kilograms. Letter writers were cautioned by the postal department to use the very thinnest paper possible and to "fold the letter in a way that will make it unnecessary to use an envelope," so that the load could be made lighter.

Gambetta's highly publicized and successful flight to the provinces gave a great impetus to balloon communications. A large crowd came to see him off, and shouts of "Long live the Republic!" followed him into the air. A voyage in a balloon was not to be taken lightly in these early days of aerial travel, and, while the sources differ as to whether Gambetta was livid or pale with fear, they agree that he did display some emotion. But, as one staunch republican paper explained, his emotion was not caused by any fears as to the aerial route, "but because he abandoned isolated and besieged Paris."

Another famous aerial voyage undertaken during the siege, but one not closely related to the military situation, was that of Janssen, the astronomer. Janssen carried all his astronomical apparatus with him in order to take observations of an expected eclipse of the sun in Algeria. Unfortunately, the balloon landed at St. Nazaire, "and just at the moment M. Janssen set foot on the ground, a gust of wind shook the basket and broke all the instruments of observation."

The success which greeted most of the balloon flights meant that the number of those people who wanted to confide themselves to balloon journeys constantly grew. Requests for missions in the provinces became more numerous as life in the besieged city became more difficult, and the government had to make out a list of priorities. This number did not decrease appreciably when some balloons were lost at sea or to the enemy, and when one even drifted as far away as Norway.

Gambetta's balloon landed at Montdidier, and he immediately dispatched a carrier pigeon, which had been carried in the balloon with him, to Paris to tell the news of his safe arrival. The use of pigeons to return news to Paris was increasingly resorted to during the siege, for balloons lacked any method of steering which could be used to return them to the capital. True, Dûpuy de Lome had been commissioned to conduct experiments on the problem of directing balloons, but his experiments dragged out over such a long period that it was obvious that nothing practical could be achieved in that direction during the siege. This did not prevent other savants from applying their minds to the same difficulty. One pupil at the Ecole Polytechnique even claimed that with four large birds he could take a balloon anywhere and bring it back again. His proposed method was to sit in a balloon gondola with a long pole, at the end of which would be placed a piece of raw meat, on which four eagles tied to the balloon would endeavor to pounce. The holder of the stick then had merely to keep pointing the meat in the direction of the course he desired to take. Nothing more was heard of this scheme, perhaps because its originator failed to accompany it with a method for obtaining a sufficient supply of eagles. And, after all, perhaps the eagles would not have approved of the scheme, for the Imperial eagles had certainly been treated somewhat shabbily recently.

Realizing that balloons were impractical for getting messages back into Paris, the government had sought about for other methods. It was thought that perhaps isolated messengers, daring individuals, might succeed in breaking through the Prussian lines. Of more than one hundred messengers of that type, only ten re-entered Paris. Shepherd dogs were also tried; six were sent into the provinces by balloon, but only one returned, and it without dispatches. The water route was also considered in connection with this problem. Hollow zinc balls filled with dispatches were to float down the Seine and be caught by properly placed nets, but this failed because of the ice on the river during the winter months. The ice also prevented the use of small iron tubes, ballasted so they would not show above the surface, which were to float down the Seine and be picked up by a barrier furnished with iron magnets.

It was to the aerial way that the French had to return to get messages back to Paris. Pigeons provided the second half of the round trip, and, although their carrying power was limited, microscopic photography came to their aid and enabled them to carry a large quantity of messages. All told, 363 pigeons were taken out of Paris by balloon; 61 did not arrive at their destination, and of the remainder only 59 returned to their dovecotes in Paris. This is not a very high percentage, but it was better than nothing. Besides, the extremely cold weather which came later during the siege made it almost impossible for the pigeons to perform their duty. To enable the pigeons to carry more messages, the famous "yes or no" dispatches came into existence, whereby Parisians sent four questions to friends or family in the provinces, who would answer "yes" or "no" in the proper order.

One interesting incident might be mentioned in connection with the homing-pigeon dispatches from the outside. The balloon "Daguerre" fell into the hands of the Prussians and with it some pigeons that were being carried out of Paris to fly messages back. These pigeons returned to Paris with dispatches indicating that Rouen had been occupied by the Germans, and that Cherbourg, Bourges, and Tours were threatened, while the rest of the country was on the verge of starvation. This attempt by the Prussians to use psychological warfare in order to sap the Parisian morale failed, because they made the mistake of signing one of the dispatches with the name of M. Lavertujon, one of the editors of the *Journal Officiel*. However, that worthy gentleman had never left Paris, and he had the pleasure of reading these dispatches over his forged signature.

Throughout the siege carrier pigeons were almost the only link of the Parisians with the outside world, so it is no wonder that the Parisians became pigeon lovers. The pigeon was looked upon as a sacred bird, and Paris shuddered with horror when it learned that the Germans had imported a number of hawks from Saxony in order to intercept the much-prized letter carriers. This worship of pigeons made them the only birds safe from being eaten by the Parisians as the siege progressed and as the food situation became worse.

For, indeed, the problem of food was beginning to take first place alongside the military situation. As the government finally reached the realization that the siege would not be over in a short time, it became imperative that genuine measures be taken to ensure the food supply. The government had dealt with it in desultory fashion before, but by the middle of October it was obvious that the half-hearted measures hitherto employed were not adequate. One of the glaring weaknesses in the whole conduct of the siege was thus present from its very beginnings, for the government had made no efforts to count the number of people within Paris nor to ensure its provisioning to any great extent beforehand. A census had been taken in 1866, but it was rendered invalid by the large number of migrations during the war and before the siege. Thus, without any statistical bases for consumption or for the supply of comestibles on hand, the government easily fell into a miscalculation of its resources.

True, useless mouths had been invited to leave before the siege set in, in order to diminish the inactive population. But a number of inhabitants from the suburbs had streamed into the city to take refuge from the Prussians and get out of the combat zones, while about 10,000 Mobile Guard were called into the city from the provinces to aid in the defense. Furthermore, many prominent men had taken their families out of Paris but had returned to the city in time for the siege, primarily because they did not want to miss anything. In some cases, this was construed as a patriotic duty. Renan, for example, sent his children to Brittany but remained with his wife in Paris, his explanation being that he believed it a duty in such circumstances "to atone by his presence, and, impotent as it is, to maintain the little strength which one has at the service of reason and country."

In addition to these inhabitants, it was calculated that there were 1,500 Americans, 40,000 Belgians, 30,000 Swiss, and 5,000 English still in Paris. All told, it was estimated before the siege that, "including the Mobiles, there are not above 1,500,000 mouths to feed, so that with proper care the supplies may be made to last for three months." No easy task that, especially if "proper care" were not taken, and certainly made no easier by the discovery, by means of a census taken on December 30, 1870—when the government finally came to the realization of the full seriousness of the predicament of Paris—that the population was 2,005,709, a figure exclusive of the armed forces.

Even before the siege had begun, indeed, even before the Empire had fallen, the price of food had increased. By the end of August, 1870, it is estimated that food was already 25 per cent dearer, for the Imperial government had not employed any maximum price legislation to accompany what it expected to be a short and victorious war. The change to a Republic did not alter the food situation materially. However, the Government of National Defense did suppress the *octroi,* the small tax on food products entering the city, because of the necessity of provisioning the capital, and shortly before the Prussians descended on Paris it had proclaimed a public hunt at Compiègne to prevent the Prussians from enjoying the game hitherto preserved for Imperial hunting pleasures. Poor people were also allowed to pick potatoes and other vegetables around Aubervilliers in order to keep them from falling into the hands of the Prussians, and all livestock in the vicinity was brought into the city. These methods did succeed in adding to the food supply of Paris, but they were done so hurriedly and in such haphazard fashion that they did not bring the necessary results. Instead, they only succeeded in deluding the Parisians with the belief that the capital was richly provisioned.

Believing the city well stocked with supplies, and having underestimated the number of people within Paris, the Parisians made another fatal error in supposing that the siege would be over in a short time—two or three months at the most—and that consequently famine was impossible. Everyone who could afford it had tried to store provisions for the siege, but even the most foresighted individuals had scarcely made provision for more than two months. The government encouraged its citizens in the belief that Paris could not be starved into submission. An announcement of September 28 had pointed out that there were 24,000 cattle, 150,000 sheep, and 6,000 hogs within Paris—a supply ordinarily enough for at least two months. Furthermore, calculating the consumption of flour at the normal peacetime rate, it was figured that there was enough on hand for a three months' supply of bread. Thus, the Parisians thought the city to be well provided with food and did not, at the beginning, think it was necessary to stint on quantity.

During the first days of October, however, panic spread through Parisian households when the butchers refused to sell more than a day's food. On October 15 began the rationing of meat which was to continue for the entire siege, the portions gradually becoming smaller and the types less choice as the siege wore on. True, some radical newspapers had suggested rationing before then, not because they believed that Paris would suffer from famine, but because they wanted a more equitable distribution of the food among the poor as well as the wealthy. This idea was not advanced because of any communistic notions of distribution and equalization of wealth; the reason given for it was that since all had to share the dangers of the siege equally it was only patriotic for all to share its privations and sufferings equally.

When the meat rationing went into effect in the middle of October, the quota of beef or mutton was set at 150 grams per person each day, and the Archbishop of Paris issued a dispensation excusing Catholics from their regular Friday fast. As the siege wore on and the supplies of cattle and sheep became exhausted, the ration was cut to 100, then 88, and eventually to 33 per day or 100 grams every three days. Finally there was none to be had, and the Parisians resorted to other types of meat.

Horses came into the Parisian diet, and their meat was sold freely and cheaply at the beginning, since the Parisians disdained this unknown food. The Horse-Eating Society at first found it necessary to inform the Parisians, by means of newspaper announcements, that horse meat was "superior to the finest beef." According to this organization, horse meat had more flavor and was more suitable to delicate stomachs than any other form of meat. Also, its fat was hailed as a good substitute for butter, which was becoming increasingly difficult to procure. It soon became unnecessary for the horse butchers to resort to such advertising, for the Parisians, deprived of their usual share of beef—and perhaps craving it all the more because of that—found it necessary to satisfy their desire for meat by resorting to horseflesh. All sorts of horses were eaten, from thoroughbred to dray, and horse meat, including that of mules and asses, underwent the same successive steps of requisitioning and rationing as did beef and mutton. From

45

valuable race horses to plow horses, they were paid for at rates varying from 1 franc 25 centimes to 1 franc 75 centimes per kilogram (i.e., approximately 12 to 18 cents per pound). Fresh horsemeat eventually disappeared from sale and reappeared only on the mornings after horses had been killed on the battlefield. In all, it was estimated that about 70,000 horses were eaten during the siege.

The requisitioning of other foodstuffs was not so successful as that of meat. Two days after the rationing of meat had begun, the requisitioning of flour, grains, and certain vegetables was decreed. But this act had as an immediate result the complete and absolute disappearance of some of the smaller hoards, such as potatoes. Dry beans, obtainable at a high price before requisitioning, disappeared from open sale once the requisitioning edict was announced. Largely because of this tendency the requisitioning of potatoes was eventually lifted, whereupon they made their reappearance—at very high prices—on the market.

While the system of requisitioning and rationing applied only to certain items in the Parisian diet, it still represented a gigantic administrative undertaking for a government which was faced with the pressure of improvising a military defense in the midst of a war. Just as these military measures represented improvisation, so did the measures taken to secure and conserve the available food supply. The poorer elements of the population—those most likely to feel the pinch of starvation first—had appreciated this problem before the members of their government did. The articulate and politically conscious workers, through their representatives in the Central Committee of Workers, had proposed to the government as early as September 14, by means of the so-called *affiches rouges* (red posters), that all food in Paris be expropriated and equitably distributed to the citizenry. Blanqui, the aged professional revolutionary and radical, continually called for an inventory of all food and a daily distribution according to everyone's needs, with, of course, the abolition of all war profiteers. To the government, such measures smacked of dangerous radicalism, and nothing was done until circumstances and the dwindling food supply forced action to be taken.

When the government finally determined to do something further about the food situation by the establishment of municipal butcher shops and canteens, the action showed the glaring defects of a scheme which was the result of improvisation rather than following a plan which had been thought out carefully beforehand. Instead of retaining control of the rationing system, the government left the administration for the distribution of food to each of the separate municipalities making up the city.

On paper the scheme did not appear unworkable. Magnin, Minister of Agriculture and Commerce, was charged with apportioning the meat among the different mayoralties, and the butchers were organized into a syndicate, since it was impossible to deal with each shop separately. These syndicates—there was one in each arrondissement—sent delegates to the abattoir every morning, and these agents received the portion for their municipality and delivered it to the other butchers. Equal amounts were at first given to each butcher, but this proved impractical, inasmuch as each butcher did not normally use the same amount of meat. So the system was changed in an attempt to ration the butchers in proportion to the number of customers. To make matters easier and avoid long waiting in queues, the customers were given three days' supply of meat at once, and they were told at approximately what hour they could be served. Each family had to trade with a certain butcher, so he would be certain of having the right amount of meat on hand. The rationing was carried out by means of cards, each head of a household receiving a card for his family. But despite all the precautions taken, long queues formed early in the morning, and the customers had to wait from two to five hours to get their meager rations at the municipal butcher shops.

Municipal administrators thus found themselves burdened with work. Not only did they have their usual duties of registering births, marriages, and deaths, looking after the schools, and attending to various other public services, but they were also faced with problems such as rationing food, lodging refugees, and quartering soldiers and a greatly increased burden of charity.

The onset of rationing and requisitioning brought home the seriousness of the situation to those Parisians who still treated the matter of the siege lightly. Everyone could now begin to feel the effects of the siege, gastronomically if not otherwise, and it is not surprising that the closing weeks of October were marked by symptoms of mass nervousness. At the very beginning of the siege, the Parisians had armed themselves in preparation for an attack in full force by the Prussians, but when this failed to materialize at once, they suspected them of some piece of treachery or an enormous effort directed against a single point. The very calm and freedom from attack annoyed and irritated the population.

The nervousness caused by the uncertain expectation of a Prussian assault was to last throughout the siege, and it was constantly being fed by predictions as to the exact date of a Prussian attack upon the walls of the city. For example, some newspapers confidently predicted a large-scale assault for October 18 because that was the anniversary of the Battle of Leipzig in 1813, where Napoleon I had met his first great check. The apparent inaction of the Prussians in the period immediately preceding the middle of October was thus laid to the large-scale preparations which were being made for an attack on that date. Of course, the attack did not materialize, but that did nothing to abate the nervousness of the Parisians.

So nervous did the Parisians become that even an easily explainable natural phenomenon, the aurora borealis which appeared over the city on October 24, was set down at first to some device on the part of the enemy. Some supposed that all the forests round the city had been set afire simultaneously in the hope of roasting or smoking the Parisians into surrender, while the more mystically inclined read in the streaking lights across the sky a Heaven-sent sign of deliverance. The tension of expectation and the baffling uncertainty that pervaded Paris were a strain on both moral and physical energy, but, lacking the scientific skepticism of the men of the twentieth century, the Parisians failed to detect any "flying saucers" or "flying disks" to add to their nervousness.

Instead, the Parisians found an outlet in the hunt for spies, which at times became a veritable mania. The police and the National Guard, as nervous as the rest of the population, saw a spy on every corner, and it was considered quite a feat to be able to arrest one. The mania of "spies" and "signalers" raged for some time. Every foreigner was suspect, and the most innocent actions might sometimes cause him to be denounced as a spy and to spend long hours in the police station explaining his actions. The possession of identification papers and genuine passes granted by the authorities were of no help whatsoever, for they were attributed to Prussian cunning.

Coexistent with the spy mania there was a craze of mistaking any light in an upper-story window at night for a signal to the enemy. This led to many unwarranted disturbances of individuals and to ludicrous incidents. But such was the ardor behind this spy hunt that it was thought better to incriminate two innocent people than to let one guilty person escape. In addition to this, there were many anecdotes of German spies, dressed in French uniforms, visiting the detached forts and ramparts. Some of these may have been fabricated by journalists eager to foster the popular mania, or they may have been the work of people misled by too active imaginations and too great patriotic ardor. There can be no mistaking the sincerity of those attempting to point out the spy danger; they were victims of the war hysteria in which one prevalent belief was that spying was an essentially Prussian occupation.

By the end of October the nerves of the Parisians were somewhat frayed. The inactivity of the Prussian besiegers made them worry, and the inactivity of the Parisian defenders made them suspicious of their own military leaders. Coupled with this there was a lack of information as to what was happening outside, and there was the distressing knowledge that rationing had to be resorted to inside the city. When this uncertainty and suspicion were given added impetus by a series of events which occurred at the end of the month, the nervousness was bound to eventuate in a series of dramatic actions.

The first in the series of events which brought matters to a climax was a headline in the newspaper *Le Combat* that Metz had fallen. Metz, considered one of the strongest fortresses of France, was under the command of Marshal Bazaine, who had led Napoleon III's Mexican expedition and who was one of the most famous of the Imperial generals. Every Parisian knew that the fall of Metz would be a disaster of the first water, because it would indicate that even the most thoroughly prepared of strongholds could not withstand the Prussian attack, and also because it would release, for use elsewhere, many thousands of German troops who had been tied up by the siege of the city and would represent the loss of a great many French troops and materiel. The effect on morale in Paris of the surrender of Metz would have been a tremendous blow, and the government hastened to deny the news of the fall of the border strong point.

In truth, the government had not yet been officially apprised of the capitulation of Metz. All that it knew was that Bazaine's aide-de-camp had left Metz to confer with the German commander regarding surrender, but it had as yet no information regarding the outcome of these negotiations. However, Trochu had informed Rochefort, who was also a member of the government, of these negotiations, and the latter had informed his radical friend Flourens. Flourens had immediately gone to the radical republican Félix Pyat, editor of *Le Combat*, and informed him of what had taken place. Without waiting for an official pronouncement on this subject, Pyat decided to publish his "scoop," and on October 27 his paper appeared with a headline reading, "Fall of Metz." The article asked if it were true that the government held a dispatch announcing that Marshal Bazaine had surrendered Metz, the implication being that the city had already fallen and that the Government of National Defense was withholding information from its citizens.

The government, of course, denied this story the very next day, October 28. Indeed, it was not until the day after the publication of the article in *Le Combat* that the capitulation of Metz was actually signed by Bazaine and Prince Charles, so the government cannot be held accountable for not having announced Bazaine's surrender the day before it occurred. The official news finally reached

Paris, and on October 31 the government issued an announcement of the fall of the citadel. Technically the government had told the truth all along, but even the most plausible explanations were ineffectual in the face of the storm of public indignation which arose over this belated confirmation of the surrender of Metz. The acknowledgment of the city's fall appeared to confirm Pyat's implied allegation that the government had withheld news and had then attempted to lie to its citizens by denying as false what a few days later it announced as true. This incident, then, not only shocked the Parisians because of the military misfortune which had occurred, but also it rightly shook their confidence in the honesty and integrity of the government which was supposed to defend their city.

But the official announcement of the fall of Metz was not the only shattering blow to which the Parisians were subjected on October 31. For at the same time came news of the return of Thiers to Paris, his diplomatic mission of securing aid for France from the courts of Europe having failed. The Parisians now realized that, despite the change from the hated Empire, they still could not hope for help from the outside world. Furthermore, rumors spread that Thiers had returned to enter into peace negotiations with Bismarck. The government had met on October 30 and had spent the night deliberating, reaching the conclusion that the time was ripe for an armistice based upon the reprovisioning of Paris. It was felt that no aid could be expected from armies which had perished at Sedan and Metz or which the amateur Gambetta was endeavoring to re-form on the Loire without trained cadres and without adequate materiel. The consensus was that this series of misfortunes could be ended only by an armistice as the first step on the road to peace, and that peace terms could be decided on by a national assembly which would be elected during the period of the armistice. It was further believed that the Prussian court would now be favorably inclined toward such an armistice, for the fatigue of the German troops plus the unexpected resistance of Paris, which might continue for another few months, would incline the Prussians to the belief that they might as well end it now. In addition, it was hoped that the pressure of Europe, exerting itself in behalf of such peace negotiations, and especially the pressure of Russia, somewhat alarmed at this sudden upsetting, to her relative disadvantage, of the balance of power in Europe, would act to give France the least disadvantageous terms for peace at this time.

When the government made its decision to send Thiers to treat with Bismarck on October 31, it did not realize that there were many Parisians who did not believe that it was necessary as yet to begin negotiations. After all, the government had been feeding "victory" propaganda to its citizens in order to keep up their morale, and the population was not able to make the quick mental transition from the idea of victory to the idea of defeat implied in the armistice negotiations. Inasmuch as some, if not most, of the members of the National Defense Government had realized the futility of fighting for victory after the defeat at Sedan, the idea of an armistice did not appear repugnant to them. The military leaders, headed by Trochu, had never believed that the defense of Paris was much more than a "heroic folly," necessary only to preserve honor. Now that Paris had not succumbed in six weeks, it was felt that honor had been sufficiently preserved; the time had come to look to the bare military facts as the basis for further action. But the people of Paris had not been told that the defense of Paris was merely an act of madness dedicated to the maintenance of French honor. To them, the defense of Paris was the preliminary to beating the

Prussian invaders off French soil. They were psychologically unprepared to accept the idea of an armistice at this time, for they could not yet bring themselves to believe that all was lost. So the rumors—true, of course—that Thiers was off to negotiate an armistice added to the general dismay caused by the government's inept handling of the news from Metz.

But that was not all. October 31 marked a threefold visitation of disaster upon the Parisian populace. It was not enough that on that date they discovered that the government had been somewhat less than open and aboveboard with them on the matter of Metz, nor that the government seemed about to betray them by entering into armistice negotiations with the enemy. For October 31 also marked the announcement of the defeat of Paris' first large-scale attempt against the Prussians who besieged the city.

It must be remembered that since the investment of the city in the middle of the preceding month, fighting had been minor and localized. The Prussians had not stormed the city as expected, and the fighting had been in the nature of small local conflicts at various points. By the close of October the French thought their military preparations adequate to attempt a large-scale offensive designed to break the investing circle. On October 28 the attack had been launched, with the Francs-tireurs de la Presse capturing le Bourget. The government had announced this news, and there was great joy in Paris, but it was premature. On October 29 the Prussians began a large-scale artillery assault upon their former positions, and on October 30 they launched a counteroffensive which succeeded in retaking le Bourget. This news was also announced on October 31, and it represented a tremendous letdown after the hopes inspired by the publication of the success of the original French attack.

At the same time that the government made known this defeat on October 31, it also published the official news of the capitulation of Metz by Bazaine and the news of the arrival of Thiers in Paris, with the public, of course, deriving the implication that the diplomat had returned to enter into armistice negotiations. These three pieces of news could not fail to arouse great emotion in Paris, especially in those quarters where there still remained a fervent belief in the triumph of Paris under the banner of the Republic.

When the disastrous news became known throughout the city, several hundred people assembled on the square in front of the City Hall, the headquarters of the government. This appears to have been a spontaneous gathering, and the main object of its participants was to find out what action the government intended to take and, if possible, to make known their opposition to any armistice at this time and their determination to fight to the bitter end. Most of the radical newspapers had already appeared with articles denouncing the government's "defeatist" stand, and the radical leaders had issued statements calling for the pursuit of a more energetic policy in carrying on the war. The mayor of the 6th arrondissement, for example, had issued a proclamation demanding that the government refuse an armistice and decree a *levée en masse* of the Parisians, or else resign. Charles Délescluze, one of the leaders of the Revolution of 1848 and still an ardent republican radical, demanded the courtmartial of Trochu and his staff as a preliminary to a new policy for carrying on the defense of Paris. Victory could be won, according to this firebrand, by the *levée en masse,* an appeal to all the peoples of the world for their assistance, the organization of the Commune of Paris along the lines of the militarily successful French Revolutionary Commune, and, in general, a policy of *défense à outrance*—fighting to the last ditch.

With talk such as this circulating through the city, the members of the government suspected a gathering storm, and the crowd in front of the City Hall was harangued by several ministers of the government. By 2 o'clock in the afternoon, the crowd's anger was diminishing, and it was on the verge of dispersing, for it lacked any central core of leadership or direction. But just at that time several battalions of the National Guard led by some of the most outspoken radical leaders arrived on the scene. The leaders of this group included men such as Blanqui and Flourens— men who were determined that Paris should not surrender at this juncture but fight to the last ounce of her strength. They were certain that victory could yet be won under the shield of the Republic. These men did not stop to listen to any pretty speeches from the members of a government which they thought had lied to them and which was now engaged in betraying Paris to the enemy. After all, how could one believe the word of men who had just denied the fact that Metz had fallen and then, two days later, admitted that it had?

Leading their men into the City Hall, these patriots decided to take forcible possession of the government from the men who pursued what they considered a traitorous policy. The regular members of the government were made prisoner, while the leaders of the radicals sought to organize a new government of active defense. Lists for a new government were hurriedly drawn up. The names included Blanc, Pyat, Victor Hugo, Dorian, Ledru-Rollin, Blanqui, and Délescluze. Indeed, it seemed almost as if 1848 were being repeated, because these men were simply the leaders of the radical republican party which had taken the leadership temporarily in 1848. Their radical republicanism had suffered no diminution through the years, and now they were being called upon to head a new government which would free France from the Prussian invaders.

While these lists were being prepared, Flourens walked back and forth across the green baize cover of the council room table, issuing orders right and left in his best imitation of a military commander. Blanqui busied himself with writing one decree after another: an order to close all the gates of the city and prevent any communications which would inform the enemy of the political changes going on in Paris; an order to the commandants of the forts to watch and repulse with energy any attacks made by the Prussians; an invitation to other heads of National Guard battalions to assemble and lead their troops to the City Hall and put them at the disposal of the new government; and an order to those battalions still waiting outside the City Hall to enter the building immediately in order to guard the doors and protect the interior of the building. Meanwhile, the crowd outside the building, steadily growing larger as the news of the events inside spread throughout the city, stood around shouting, "No armistice!" "Resistance to death!" "Long live the Republic!" and other patriotic slogans.

But while all this was going on, two members of the Government of National Defense, Picard and Ferry, managed to escape from the room in which they had been imprisoned, and they hurried to sound the alarm, to organize the Mobile Guard for the relief of their imprisoned comrades, and to summon several battalions of the National Guard of whose loyalty they could be assured. It was the 106th Battalion of the National Guard which came to the rescue of the government and finally succeeded during the course of the evening in chasing Flourens and his partisans away and delivering the Government of National Defense by 3 o'clock in the morning. No actual fighting took place; the adherents of Flourens melted away when members of the 106th Battalion succeeded in gaining entrance to the City Hall. As soon as they found themselves outnumbered, Flourens' troops disappeared, though not without first exacting a promise that none of the leaders of the insurrectionary attempt would be prosecuted and not without hearing a guarantee by the government to hold elections to determine the future of the government and its policies. At the same time they reassured the citizens who waited outside of the desire of the Government of National Defense to protect the patriotic interests of France.

In the light of what happened some six months later, historians have tended to look upon this turbulent day of October 31 as a harbinger of the social revolution to come, which manifested itself in the Commune of Paris in 1871. The only thing wrong with such an interpretation is that it involves a misinterpretation of the Commune, which we shall discuss later, and it does not fit the facts of the day of October 31. Although some Parisians doubtless believed that the insurrection of October 31 had been carefully prepared in advance and was part of a gigantic scheme of the radicals toward a "red" revolution, this is belied by the events themselves. Even General Trochu agreed that this abortive attempt to place a new government at the helm was not born of a conspiracy, but rather had developed spontaneously from the sadness and anger of the people at the disastrous news which had broken upon their illusions at one fell swoop. The population, angered by the triple visitation of disaster involved in the fall of Metz, the return of Thiers for armistice talks, and the failure of the sortie at le Bourget, had gathered for no express purpose but to make known its desire to continue the struggle. Flourens and his National Guard, predominantly from the working-class district of Belleville, had taken advantage of a situation which was not of their creation. The unplanned aspects of the whole affair are shown by the fact that the armed insurrectionists were so few and that they did not quite know what to do when they had achieved a partial success. Flourens' ironic remark demonstrates the spontaneous nature of the uprising and gives the lie to those who claimed that the "reds" were well prepared with arms, troops, and leaders: "The recapture of the City Hall was the only military operation in which Trochu succeeded during the whole siege—20,000 soldiers against 400 republicans!" [1]

The activities of the insurrectionists themselves indicate that they were primarily interested in resistance to the Prussians rather than in any reorganization of society along social lines at this time. Blanqui, the "red bogeyman" of the upper classes, had occupied himself with writing decrees designed to strengthen Paris' defense rather than to strip the possessing classes of their property. The shibboleths of the crowd were for stronger elements of resistance and not for any radical reorganization of society. The call for the Commune which had been heard did not mean communism, but rather a return to the system of municipal elections and the placing of the national government in the hands of the municipal representatives of Paris, as had been done during the First Republic, under whose aegis that Republic had won such outstanding victories. Certainly the cry for a *levée en masse* was derived directly from the legends woven about the armies of the First Republic.

One thing is certain. This was not a disloyal mob which had attempted to change the government of the country

---

[1] Gustave Flourens, *Paris Livré* (3d ed.; Paris, 1871), p. 154.

through insurrection. It was not in favor of an armistice; in fact, the mob was so loyal that they looked upon the members of the Government of National Defense as being only lukewarm in their patriotism as compared with the masses. They were determined to save Paris, and, if necessary, to make their leaders follow them along those lines, or to get a new set of leaders who would. Fortified with myths, they forgot the need for guns to achieve victory.

Two things were accomplished by the night of October 31: it ruled out the possibility of an armistice in the near future, and it strengthened rather than weakened the government of Trochu. In a plebiscite held on November 3, the people of Paris overwhelmingly "approved" the Government of National Defense by a vote of 557,996 to 62,-638. But it cannot be said that this vote was indicative of the real Parisian sentiment, for, like the Napoleonic plebiscite on the Liberal Empire, this plebiscite did not admit of a fair choice. It did not show that Paris approved of Trochu and his colleagues any more than it showed that the capital rejected the ideas of Blanqui, Flourens, Pyat, or the other radical republican leaders, although some people claimed that it was a vote for the men of moderation and order against the partisans of social revolution. But the choice was not so clear as all that, and the government claimed that it stood for the defense of France just as much as did the radicals. Nor did all the people who voted for the government do so unqualifiedly; a great part of those who voted "yes" believed that it was necessary to support the government for a time, and that the government had not yet been given enough chance to demonstrate either its ability or debility. Still others felt that an affirmative vote should be given if only to show the Prussians that unanimity reigned in Paris and that the Parisians remained united in the face of the foreign invader.

Furthermore, some of the radical republican supporters felt obliged to vote "yes" because a "no" vote might be interpreted as favoring peace rather than a continuation of the struggle.

October 31 was thus chiefly responsible for continuing the fatuous military administration of Trochu, and for letting it be thought that the confidence of the population was behind the government. Without October 31 perhaps the destructive leadership of Trochu might have been overthrown before it was too late, but the events of that day threw such a fright of disunity and internal strife into most of Paris that the government was consolidated in its position. Thus the government remained secure for three months in a public approbation which it did not deserve, for that approval rested in large measure upon the mistaken belief that the government as then constituted was the best instrument available to carry on an aggressive campaign against the besieging forces, although the government itself did not believe in the possibility or practicability of such a course. A further result of the insurrection of October 31 was the rupture of Thiers' armistice negotiations with Bismarck, who saw that internal dissension within the city provided him with a potent ally. The siege, then, was to continue.

Chapter III

Hope Revives... and Falls

Satisfied that the government was going to continue the war, public interest in the political implications of the events of October 31 soon abated. Some of the principal actors in the affair were arrested, despite a "deal" which had been made with the members of the government, but most of these were later released, and no large-scale prosecutions ensued. All of this was done without too much ado; the Parisians seemed to be more occupied with the care of their stomachs, as the lengthening of the siege made them tighten their belts, than with political questions.

As the stock of provisions became scantier, the Parisians began to turn to new and strange dishes which were not normally included in their diet. Dogs, cats, and rats began to be eaten freely. The dogs and cats had wandered around the streets, but their presence soon excited recrimination and wants. Furthermore, the feeding of them soon became a social question, and earlier in the siege people had already begun to complain about these "useless mouths." Owners of pets had to keep constant guard over them, for regular hunts against domestic animals were undertaken. The price of rats soon became so high that not everyone was able to afford them; the market rats were considered of the highest quality since they had been nourished on a diet of cheese and grain. Although some people could not stomach any of these animals, there were some who ate them because there was nothing else to be obtained, while still others even acquired a taste for them, finding that cat resembled rabbit and that rats tasted somewhat like birds.

The animals in the Jardin des Plantes and the Jardin d'Acclimitation also represented a source of meat which could not be overlooked, especially since it was difficult to provide them with food. Those considered most precious were saved until the last, and the only ones sold for food were those species of which they had two. Eventually, however, this principle of selection had to be disregarded in the face of the diminishing food supply. Even Castor and Pollux, the elephants who were the pride of the Paris zoo and the two most popular animals in the city, had to be sacrificed because they represented "such a great quantity of digestible (!) meat." Because of the difficulty of approaching them, the lions and tigers were spared, and their cages were protected against bombardment in order not to let loose a flood of wild animals on Paris in case a Prussian shell should find its mark. The anthropoids, too, were not killed, perhaps from some vague Darwinian notion that they were the relatives of the people of Paris and eating them would be tantamount to cannibalism.

However, the supply of such exotic foodstuffs was limited, and it is in the realm of ordinary groceries that the privations of the Parisians during the siege can be traced, for such foods either reached scandalously high prices or were not to be obtained at any price. Cheese, for example, was a favorite with the Parisians, but it had disappeared from the ordinary channels of trade. Potatoes cost twenty times as much as in the preceding year, while olive oil more than doubled in price, and eggs went from fifteen centimes to two francs apiece. Other foods showed even higher rises in price: geese from seven to eighty francs, turkeys from ten to ninety, and so on.

The siege caused a serious situation in regard to milk. In ordinary times, Paris consumed 800,000 liters of milk per day, 600,000 of which came from the provinces. The siege cut down this supply by nine-tenths, since the Parisians had to depend upon the milk furnished by the cows brought into the city, and the productivity of those animals declined because of the lack of forage. A wet-nurse service was instituted to take care of infants because of the lack of fresh milk.

Some foodstuffs, however, were never lacking. Mustard, for example, was always plentiful; there was no meat to put it on! Wine, too, was always abundant, but beer was scarce because Paris was cut off from the normal Alsatian and German supply. An attempt was made to brew some beer in Paris, but the necessary ingredients were lacking, and this *ersatz* product was a failure. Wine and mustard can hardly be said to be very nourishing, despite any effect they might have in stimulating the palate or other appetites, and of food having a high nutritive value—the type necessary for sustaining life and fighting a war—there was only a limited supply. No food that could possibly be utilized was allowed to be wasted. Frequent instructions were given to the populace on how to keep bread fresh for a long time and how rotten peas and potatoes could be turned to use.

The shortage of foods was further aggravated by the profit-making propensities of the Parisian traders in foodstuffs. Fraudulent exploitation by adulteration was one source of profit to those who did not hesitate to make fortunes at the expense of their fellow citizens. Chemistry reassumed its ancient status of alchemy, although this time its endeavors were to make base foods into high-priced edibles. Squash was doctored and converted into apricot marmalade, and carrots were cunningly transmuted into quince or pineapple jelly. Furthermore, when beef had become an unknown quantity in the Parisian world, the same merchants were still selling beef sausages at six francs a pound, although even the most gullible would have hesitated to equate their contents with beef.

As if this were not enough, the market men were demanding the most extortionate prices for everything that was edible, and they refused to make the least concession to the starving populace. All articles of food not regulated by government price-fixing measures were up to extraordinary figures, and rationed foods were available at black-market prices. The restaurateurs and food traders thus became fat while the people became thin, and this at the expense of a shortage of food that was often more apparent than real. Food hoarding was, of course, a common procedure, as may be seen by the fact that food came out of hiding when Thiers returned to Paris at the end of October, his arrival being the occasion for a universal rumor that there would soon be an armistice which would allow for the reprovisioning of Paris. The price of butter dropped sharply from twenty to six francs but rose again when it was learned that Bismarck, knowing of the events of October 31, had refused the armistice. The commission men were furious at having lowered their prices even for three days.

The scarcity of food was bound to cast suspicion on the strangers in the midst of the Parisian populace who were a drain upon the food supply without contributing in some measure to the defense. Thus, the many foreigners resident in Paris began to feel uncomfortable, for they were classed as "useless mouths" along with the cats, dogs, and other domestic pets. Paris felt that owing to the exigencies of the siege it must temporarily give up its role as hostess to the world, and the large foreign colony which inhabited Paris was politely asked to leave after diplomatic negotiations had ensured their safe passage through the investing circle. Some foreigners had already left Paris in the period immediately preceding the siege, and a second exodus was organized in the middle of November.

It cannot be said that the feelings of the foreigners were hurt by this polite invitation to leave. The food situation within Paris was such that many foreigners welcomed a chance to return to a normal diet by abandoning the besieged capital. Besides, the Parisians were beginning to display unwonted signs of animosity toward perfectly innocuous foreigners as well as toward the hated Prussians. Disappointed by the neutrality of the great powers, the French were also angered by the treatment of their nation in foreign newspapers, especially the London *Times*. Since the French were extremely sensitive in regard to the diplomatic isolation into which Bismarck had maneuvered them, even the charitable acts performed by the British during the war could not mitigate the Anglophobia. Colonel Loyd-Lindsay, for example, arrived in Paris in mid-October with a gift of 500,000 francs for treatment of the French wounded, the money having been raised by popular subscription in England. But inasmuch as the English showed their neutrality by donating an equal amount to the Prussians, the gift served in no way to diminish the bitter feeling against the English. When another Englishman, Richard Wallace, was generous with his gifts, the French were quite pleased, but their thanks were to Wallace as an individual, not to the English people as a whole —a distinction made possible because Wallace was the illegitimate son of the late Lord Hertford by an actress, which of course meant that he could not be considered fully representative of Victorian England.

The Americans were somewhat better liked by the French. For one thing, the American people and government had been quick to greet the new sister Republic. In addition, the Americans in Paris had set up a hospital for the wounded which was one of the best in Paris, for it drew upon the experience acquired during the American Civil War and it possessed the American love of efficiency and sanitation. Motivated by humanitarian instincts, the Americans still wished to remind the French, in words that have a familiar ring, that they "had not forgotten and would not ignore the relief extended to us during our struggle for independence—that the great and good work of Lafayette and his *confrères* was still fresh in the memory of all true Americans." [1]

Some of the foreigners in Paris endeavored to help the French by participation in actual combat activities. Realizing that every civilized man has two countries—his own and France—they had organized a legion called the "Friends of France," which fought alongside the regular troops throughout the siege. But most of the foreigners confined themselves to noncombatant humanitarian services, such as the American ambulance service.

Indeed, the service of hospitals and ambulances, whether by natives or foreigners, was one of the most prominent aspects of military activities during the siege. Three separate divisions comprised the ambulance service of the army of Paris. There were the regular military ambulances, sadly inadequate and inefficient; the ambulances of the Société Internationale de Génève (the Red Cross), to which

---

[1] Thomas W. Evans, *History of the American Ambulance Established in Paris during the Siege of 1870–71* (London, 1873), p. 669.

were attached the American and Italian ambulances; and, finally, the ambulances of the Press, a result of individual and collective charity efforts.

Besides these worthwhile and legitimate ambulance and hospital services, there were many others—too many, in fact—that were not worthy of the name, which were set up by publicity-seeking individuals or organizations. The plethora of ambulances was so great that patients were actually touted for, and unemployed ambulance vans were in such profusion that department stores, such as the Magasins du Louvre and other similar establishments, delivered their purchases in vehicles bearing the Red Cross insignia. Since the number of skirmishes and, hence, of the wounded, was smaller than had been expected, there was real competition on the battlefield, not so much to minister to the suffering as to fill ambulances.

This ambulance craze was one which the women of Paris carefully fostered. Nurses' uniforms set the pace in feminine styles, and the hospitals were tended mostly by young girls and actresses, perhaps not so much for patriotic and humanitarian reasons as for the amorous diversions which nursing afforded. Certain it is that many such hospitals wanted only "interesting wounded," young officers, the most agreeable and pleasant to nurse. In addition, many of the romantic young ladies made it a point to drive about Paris, elegantly dressed in somber clothing and rolling bandages at the windows of their carriages, so that no one could possibly miss their display of patriotism.

The wounded man was much more than an object of fashion; he was also an object of utility. If one could be so fortunate as to secure the presence of a wounded man in one's home, this would save one from the unpleasantness of having some of the refugees from the suburbs quartered there, and it was further believed that he could save one, in case of future necessity, from incendiarism, pillage, and Prussian requisition. In addition, many able-bodied "slackers" found jobs in hospitals so that they would not have to face danger elsewhere, and their presence was a scandal which aroused many people to protest.

However, not all the ambulance work was a matter of fashion or diversion. Much of it was a hard, smelly task, and there were many and notable exceptions to the young ladies who merely dallied with their nursing duties. Foremost among the exceptions were the Sisters of Charity and many of the better class of actresses who threw themselves into this work without any consideration of its lighter aspects. Indeed, anyone who is familiar with the patriotic zeal displayed by the women of Paris during the French Revolution would not have been surprised to see the response of their great-granddaughters of 1870 when *la Patrie* was endangered.

There can be no doubt that the women suffered much and worked bravely for the defense of Paris. Many of them were left without funds or employment as their husbands had been taken prisoner during the great French defeats and as many of the clothing shops in which they worked had been shut down. The Parisian women were jealous of the role which they might play in the defense of the city. On the afternoon of October 7, for example, about 150 women marched to the City Hall carrying Red Cross flags and asking the government to replace men by women in the ambulance service in order to increase the number of men available for combat duty. This manifestation, as all the others, was favorably received by a member of the government, and the women retired singing patriotic songs. Despite the fact that many women, chiefly those of the upper classes or the romantically inclined young ladies, did ambulance work for social reasons, there can be little doubt that many *Parisi-*

ennes did valuable work in tending the sick and wounded.

Another aspect of the war work of women was the occupation of *vivandière* or *cantinière*. These women, decked out in rather theatrical costumes, formed part of each battalion of National Guard, and their duty was to provide refreshment for the soldiers, much as the Salvation Army "lassies" did during World War I and the Red Cross girls during World War II. In some cases their care for the soldiers seems to have gone beyond that ordinarily expected of Salvation Army or Red Cross workers, however. Although, theoretically, only married women were permitted to function as "daughters of the regiment," in actual practice many of these camp followers were young girls, so the guardians of public morals frequently inveighed against this practice which exposed young ladies to temptation while away from parental supervision.

Some attempts were even made to have the women take an active part in the fighting. Such was Félix Belly's project for a battalion of female soldiers to be called "The Amazons of the Seine." Belly was a crank, a member of the "lunatic fringe" of society, who had already achieved some measure of notoriety for his espousal of the idea that all the misfortunes of the French might be attributed to their love of tobacco. His scheme for feminine fighters proved no more successful than his attempt to make the French give up smoking. But, judging from the appearance of the women who responded to his call, it is quite possible that had the Amazonian battalion gone into action, its looks would have frightened the Prussians much more than the fighting done by the male defenders of Paris.

Although the women of France did not possess the right of suffrage during the nineteenth century, they always played an active role in political life. This was especially the case during the siege. A feminine journal was founded, and some women were regular attendants at the meetings of the political clubs with which Paris abounded. However, it is questionable whether the presence of the women at the club sessions was as indicative of their interest in political activities as it was of their desire to gather some warmth and break the monotony of existence. Certainly not all the women could be so active in political and social work as was Mme Edmond Adam, the wife of the first Prefect of Police in the Government of National Defense. She organized the ambulance at the Music Conservatory and worked there almost constantly, but she also found time to conduct a salon attended by the most noteworthy republican politicians of the time; and when the siege was over she wrote an interesting account of it under the name of Juliette Lamber.

Not all the women were so fortunate as Madame Adam, who was able to exhibit her patriotic ardor and still maintain some semblance of family life during the siege. The war inevitably kept many families apart, but even when the husbands remained in Paris the siege cannot be said to have favored a normal family life. For one thing, many of the proletariat quit their jobs in the factories or shops, some of which had shut down anyhow, and joined the National Guard. There they received a stipend of 1 franc 50 centimes per day, hardly enough to provide for a family. Although the workers could have received from three to six francs per day in private industry, especially those heavy industries converted to armament factories, they considered it more dignified to scorn these jobs and to throw a gun on their shoulders and mount guard on the ramparts. Inasmuch as many families were reduced to poverty by this patriotic gesture on the part of the family breadwinner, the government soon decreed that wives of the National Guard should receive half-pay—75 centimes per day.

This gave an impetus to family life in the poorer classes

in a rather curious way, for there now began to be a large number of marriages of people living at the same address. The explanation of this social phenomenon is that many people who had been living together without benefit of clergy and were considered by their neighbors to be model husband and wife suddenly found it to their advantage to sanctify their relations by becoming married. To those romantic souls who would prefer a less materialistic explanation of these marriages, it might be pointed out that the view taken by some conservative moralists was simply that the husband, involved in defending the city, took the precaution of marrying his wife in order to leave his name and legal rights to her and the children in case of death while fighting for his country. Whatever be the explanation, and although these legitimizations may be viewed as merely a nominal change in the family relationship, they must certainly be considered as a triumph for official morality. Félix Pyat did not even want these marriages *à quinze sous* (so called for the 75 centimes which wives of men of the National Guard received) to be that. He demanded that the indemnity be given to unmarried "wives," for, like a good radical, he opposed religious marriage and its prohibition of divorce.

Of course Pyat was no different from the other republican radicals who seized the opportunity granted them by the complete absence of censorship after September 4 to display the anticlericalism typical of French republicanism since the days of the French Revolution. Inasmuch as the Empire had, in many respects, followed a policy favorable to the Church, the reaction to the Empire after Sedan also involved an attack upon the Church, or at least the freedom to make such an attack in the radical newspapers and clubs which were now given free rein.

72

The downfall of the Imperial protector, however, did not mean that the clergy would refuse to assist the new government in any way. As a matter of fact, the clergy performed useful patriotic as well as humanitarian services throughout the war and siege. The first and most obvious aspect of their war work was acting as chaplains to the armed forces. Each of the twenty-one forts which surrounded and protected Paris received a chaplain. Besides celebrating the Mass and administering the last rites, the clergy also endeavored to use this opportunity "to make Christian sentiments penetrate to the hearts" of the soldiers, a somewhat thankless task not always accompanied with success. Not only did the clergy act as religious guides to the soldiers, but they also offered their quarters to be used as barracks and hospitals. By far the greatest service performed by the priests during the siege was the work they did in the ambulances, the Frères des Ecoles Chrétiennes being especially noteworthy in that respect.

Another service performed by a religious order, and one which seems quite far afield from the saving of souls or of lives, was the care of the semaphore system within Paris. This was taken over by the Jesuits, who also directed the nocturnal telegraphic service between the forts.

Despite the fine work done by the priests during the siege, this does not mean that criticism of the Church was lessened thereby. The radical republicans demanded suppression of the *budget des cultes* (the financial aid given by the state to the Church), the melting of the church bells as had been done during the French Revolution, and combat military service for the priests. This last demand disregarded the fact that the priests alleviated much suffering during the siege by performing good works, some of it right at the front lines, and the further fact that the priests would not have provided a very substantial contribution to the fighting force inasmuch as 612 out of the 1,015 priests in Paris were already over forty-five years of age.

Several incidents bring out clearly the anticlericalism of the radical republicans. In the 11th arrondissement, Mayor Mottu, thoroughly imbued with the anticlerical spirit of the French Revolution, replaced all the clerical instructors in the schools by lay teachers and cut off the pay of the clerics. He also kept the priests out of the ambulances in his arrondissement, and they were allowed in only when a dying soldier asked for them to perform the last rites. Actions such as this would seem to give some substance to the complaint of the outstanding ultramontane layman of the time, Veuillot, that the Government of National Defense was giving its tacit support to religious persecution. Actually, the government was almost powerless in such cases, but it cannot be said that it was consciously following an anticlerical policy, as can be judged by looking at its composition. There is no doubt that the freedom of speech and assembly brought in by the Revolution of September 4 gave anticlericalism the opportunity to grow, and the anticlericals were not slow in taking advantage of this.

Blanqui's journal, *La Patrie en danger,* took the lead in presenting the extreme anticlerical viewpoint. In some of its vitriolic articles it went so far as to attempt to establish a connection between religious workers and houses of prostitution and to discredit the supporters of the Church by charging Veuillot with hypocrisy.

The defenders of the faith were not slow in answering the challenge of the reinvigorated anticlericalism. *L'Univers,* Veuillot's newspaper, traded polemics with the radical newspapers. Although it had been mildly anti-Bonapartist under the Empire, *L'Univers* was not too enthusiastic about the Government of September 4 because of the freedom which it allowed to the anticlerical radicals. The Masons, the ancient enemies of the Church, also came in for criticism by Veuillot, especially when ten Parisian Masonic lodges excommunicated King William and Prince Frederick of Prussia from the order of Freemasonry. The ultramontanes tended to look upon the war as a war of religion —Protestantism struggling against Catholicism. Viewed in that light, the taking of Rome by the Italians was a serious blow to Veuillot and the ultramontanes. The French troops which had previously held the city for the Pope and thus safeguarded it from the troops of King Victor Emmanuel had been withdrawn because of the exigencies of the war on French soil. The withdrawal of the French troops made the occupation of Rome by Italian troops possible, and on September 20 the forces of Pope Pius had surrendered the Eternal City to General Cadorna, the commander of the Italian army. Veuillot saw in this capture of Rome by the secular forces representing national unification a victory for Bismarck and the anticlericals and interpreted it as a great blow to France. To him, the territorial independence of the Pope was an adjunct of French diplomatic as well as spiritual well-being. But Paris was too busy with its own problems to seek for any hidden relationships between its own siege and political events in Rome.

As a matter of fact, all peripheral questions took second rank in the Paris mind as the month of November, 1870, passed. Even the omnipresent question of food was temporarily relegated to a minor position as, for the first time since the outbreak of the war, the military situation appeared hopeful to the Parisians. After the breakdown of armistice negotiations at the beginning of the month, the government was forced to take some decisive military steps. As long as armistice negotiations had been possible, the government, headed by military men who did not believe in a successful defense, had stalled and merely attempted to make some sort of a showing until it could honorably treat for peace. But Bismarck, aided by the red-hot patriots who had engaged in the insurrectionary activities of October 31, had closed the door on armistice negotiations for the present, so now the government had to evolve a real military policy.

The first step in this direction was an army reorganization which took place on November 10. In truth, this can hardly be called a *re*organization, for until that time very little system had existed at all. The army defending Paris consisted of many disparate troops, and very little effort had been made to weld these into an effective fighting force. Two main types of troops can be distinguished among the defenders of the city: the regular military formations and the National Guard, essentially a civilian army. Within the regular military formations there were divergences also. In the first place, there were the regular army troops, remainders of the Imperial standing army, the professional soldiers, or troops of the line, as they were called. These were the core of the fighting force, but they were relatively few. In addition, there was the Mobile Guard, made up of reservists usually of bourgeois or peasant origin, capable of competent military action. Then there were the Francs-tireurs, a romantic group of irregular volunteers, raised by private individuals, distinguished by their bravery and dash, but, by their very nature, somewhat unamenable to discipline. Finally, among the regular military forces were to be counted the sailors who had been called into Paris and whose chief duty was to man the huge guns of the fortifications.

The other great mass of men called to the defense of Paris were enrolled in the National Guard, which consisted of almost the whole of the able-bodied male population of Paris, and which represented a potential fighting force of almost 350,000 men. Most of these men had joined in response to a call by the Government of National Defense issued shortly after it had power thrust upon it. It was composed primarily of the poor, working-class population of Paris. But their object in joining it cannot be said to have been the receipt of the pay, inasmuch as pay was not authorized until after the men had joined and had found themselves without resources, since they had no savings and had left their jobs to participate in this patriotic enterprise of defending the capital.

Although these civilian soldiers were looked down upon by the regular army formations mentioned above, they were extremely enthusiastic about the part they might play in the defense. But they had little or no work to do, for they were placed under the command of the Ministry of Interior rather than the War Department, and the conservative members of the government were somewhat suspicious of this armed mob which they had created in response to the public fear that the Prussians would attempt to take the city by storm. The chief function of the Guard was to guard the immense perimeter of the ramparts which surrounded the city, and they attacked this job with great enthusiasm—with so much enthusiasm, in fact, that their commander had to issue an order begging them "not to go out with drums beating and colors flying to the outposts; a discreet reserve being required in that advanced position." But the duty of guarding the ramparts became a sinecure when it became certain that the Prussians would not try to take the city by assault. The National Guard thus became an unemployed army on duty behind a useless line of fortifications.

The effect on morale of putting men able and willing to fight on such useless duty was soon apparent. Inasmuch as not everyone was placed on this active duty at the same time, there was ample leisure for grousing of all sorts. The loose organization of the Guard, under officers elected by the men, made for a lack of discipline. Some of the men gossiped while on duty; others played cards and gambled; some visited the near-by canteens and drank *petit noir,* a mixture of brandy, coffee, and sugar; and still others were absent without leave while they resorted to the cafés in town. Drunkenness became almost the normal condition of the men at the ramparts, and in the evenings they gathered in the tents for stories and songs and still more drinking. The idleness combined with the drinking to produce constant disputes and fighting, and indiscipline was the chronic complaint of most observers. That life in the National Guard was rather soft and appealing is shown by the fact that men of the Mobile Guard of Paris continually deserted to National Guard battalions, thereby exchanging a starving and freezing life at the outposts for one at the inner ramparts where they got thirty sous a day, good rations, and little work. In this manner, the 6th, 7th, and 8th Battalions of the Parisian Mobiles, or *moblots* as they were called, had only 2,500 soldiers of the 8,000 inscribed on their lists.

In the middle of October the government had made a half-hearted attempt to select some fighting troops from the masses of the National Guard by calling for volunteers, but only 6,000 men responded. Most of the National Guard were suspicious of this attempt to select men from their ranks, and they could not understand why the organization as a whole was not employed to fight against the enemy in full force. Indeed, the National Guard had been suspicious of the government's attitude toward them from the beginning and especially suspicious of their organization under the Ministry of the Interior. This made them believe that the government intended to use them only for auxiliary police work instead of for actual defense of the city, and that was a blow to their pride. To counteract this, many of the battalions composed of proletarian fighters had elected delegates to a vigilance committee, whose duty it was to see that the fighting capacity of the Guard was not slighted by the government. These committees from the various districts had then formed a central body which took the name of the Central Committee of the Twenty Arrondissements. This action in turn inspired still more suspicion on the part of the conservative members of the government, who became afraid that the armed working class might eventually turn against the solid upholders of property and who were therefore determined not to transform the National Guard into too potent an organization. A vicious circle was thus formed, because the National Guard, neglected in this way, then became a fertile breeding ground for growing disaffection with the government's do-nothing policy.

National Guard men were thus always spoiling for a fight with the enemy. They believed in the praise which the newspapers showered upon them, especially the republican newspapers who saw in them the nearest approach to the French Revolutionary army of *sans-culottes*. It is no wonder that they acquired what some observers believed was an exaggerated opinion of their own worth. We will never know if their opinion of their fighting prowess was exaggerated or not, because they were never really given a chance to prove their mettle. They were not given the training which might have welded them into a potent fighting force, and they were employed only half-heartedly at best. As a result, members of the National Guard during the siege never had the opportunity to become disabused of the notion that they were—or could be, if given the chance—a real fighting army.

Only when the armistice negotiations had failed did the Ministry of War, always suspicious of nonprofessional soldiers, consent to measures at the beginning of November which would make the National Guard militarily effective to some slight extent. Thus, as a prerequisite to the army reorganization of November 10, four fighting, or "marching," companies were to be formed from every battalion of the National Guard, and these were to be formed into "marching" battalions, as distinct from the remaining "sedentary" or stationary battalions. This was designed to produce an effective fighting force of 100,000 men. Even this measure did not completely succeed, because the stationary battalions remained under the Interior Ministry. Clément Thomas, appointed General of the National Guard by the army reorganization, was in favor of the inclusion of the Guard in the ranks of the regulars, but the military men stubbornly refused to stake their reputations upon the military performance of a group of raw recruits, who remained raw recruits largely because the military refused to train them. As one professional soldier stated, "Two hundred thousand men would be superb if they were solid. But at the sight of the first shell half of them will bolt, and by the time the fighting has lasted five minutes, the rest will have followed." If the generals distrusted the National Guard, it is no wonder that the National Guard in its turn distrusted the generals who refused to make use of them.

Considering the varying fighting qualities of the troops available, the reorganization accomplished on November 10 was a fairly sensible arrangement, although it made no provision for further training of the National Guard to convert them into soldiers capable of carrying on the burden of genuine combat. The stationary National Guard under General Clément Thomas was to look after internal order and to man the inner circle of ramparts around the city; a second army under General Ducrot, consisting of the regular troops, the marching battalions of the National Guard, and the Mobile Guard, was to do active duty in the field; General Vinoy headed the army, including sailors, which manned the great fortresses which surrounded the city.

The army reorganization, however, was but a prelude to other and more significant military developments involved in the news of the French victory at the Battle of Coulmiers (November 9) and the retaking of the town of Orleans by the French. Out of nowhere, Gambetta, heading the Government's Delegation at Tours, had been able to organize a fighting force which had struck the first really effective French blow of the war. General Paladines, commanding the Army of the Loire, had decisively defeated General Von der Thann, who had retreated with the loss of guns and men, and the French had retaken Orleans. Not only did this give a tremendous boost to French morale—the example of Joan of Arc in the capture of Orleans was not lost upon the French public—but it also decreed a complete change in strategy for the defenders of Paris.

As we know, the Parisian military leaders had no military plans for a conclusive victory; their idea was to repulse the Germans if they attempted to take the city by storm, but outside of that they were satisfied to hold out long enough until the honor of the military had been assuaged and then seek an honorable capitulation. General von Moltke, the leader of the Prussian forces, later ascribed careful planning to the military endeavors of the defenders of Paris, probably because more honor is to be won when foresight and strategy are attributed to one's opponents, provided one is able to defeat them. Actually, however, French military efforts throughout the siege were the result of circumstances forced upon them from the outside or were due to internal political expediency, and not to any farsighted design on the part of the Parisian military leaders.

When, at the end of September, Trochu's colleagues in

the government had asked him for a realistic appraisal of the military situation, he claimed that it was "an absolute military axiom" that a fortified town could not withstand the enemy unless it were sustained by a pre-existing army, and that since there was no other French army in the field at that time, the defense of Paris was "an act of heroic folly . . . necessary to save the honor of France."[2] But Gambetta's dispatch announcing the victory of the Army of the Loire and the retaking of Orleans meant that Trochu had to revise his military calculations, for there now was a French army in the field and a successful one at that. Gambetta was now able to take the initiative and demand that the forces of Paris co-ordinate their movements with those of the armies coming to their rescue, and it was Gambetta, not Trochu nor his chief strategist and ablest military leader, Ducrot, who determined the actions of the relieving armies. Trochu could no longer remain passive; some plan had to be adopted and active military measures taken.

Not that Trochu was without help in formulating a plan. All Paris was ready and willing to give the military authorities advice on how to conduct a campaign. Every journalist "who can point a pen or shoulder a pencil" had a theory of strategy which he frequently presented to his readers. And every reader was also an authority on his own and was more than anxious to present the government with gratuitous advice. Practically all Paris seemed to be reading some sort of military manual, which, of course, constituted one as a military authority. This tremendous interest in military matters is apparent in every war, and the Parisians were not laggards in this respect. In addition to the various official military manuals which were distributed widely and read avidly, a number of cheap abridgments had been brought

---

[2] General Louis Jules Trochu, *Une Page d'histoire contemporaine devant l'Assemblée nationale* (Paris, 1871), pp. 66–67.

out, and these sold very well in Paris during the siege. So everyone felt qualified, either having read newspapers, a book, or an abridgment of one, or having enrolled in the National Guard, to give the government the benefit of his military advice.

Besides the reading matter available, the clubs presented a fertile source of military ideas to the authorities, as well as acting as political gadflies. These clubs, which constituted an important part of Parisian political and social life during the siege, also acted as breeding grounds for military strategy, especially since politics and military action soon became inextricably intertwined. These groups were far different from the fraternal and social organizations of the Second Empire which went by the name of "clubs," there being few political and literary organizations of that type. In their elementary form, the clubs of the siege had existed since the beginning of the blockade in the groups which gathered around the kiosks and the corners of the boulevards to discuss the news and perhaps listen to some self-appointed orators. It was not long before they were installed in empty concert halls and cafés, many of which the proprietors let them use in exchange for lighting and heating. With the closing of the theaters and other places of amusement at the beginning of the siege, there was very little for the people to do in their spare time, and there were enough loud voices and ideas to furnish personnel for the gatherings. Besides, the Revolutionary Era had furnished examples of the possible importance of clubs of various sorts, and it was considered proper that with the proclamation of a new Republic there should again be a concomitant growth of clubs. So fast did the idea take hold that by the beginning of October there were about thirty clubs in Paris furnishing oratorical nourishment.

The clubs generally took the names of the places where

they met, but some of them had other titles as well, which are interesting as a revelation of the hopes and state of mind of the Parisian populace. Thus we find clubs distinguished by such names as "Resistance," "Vengeance," "Deliverance," and "Country in Danger." There was a price of admission to the clubs, but this varied as much as the lighting within the auditoriums where the meetings were held. The entrance price was generally twenty-five centimes, but the Club Favié, located in the working-class district of Belleville, charged only ten centimes, while at the club of the Salle Valentino, which had a bourgeois membership, the entrance fee was as high as fifty centimes. At some clubs one gave what one pleased, and the question arose at the Club Favié—"the temple of democracy," as its adherents referred to it—whether people who could not afford to pay should be excluded from the meetings. A compromise which satisfied both principles and necessities was finally reached: people would be asked to pay, but the entrance fee would not be exacted from those who could not afford it.

Whole families attended the club meetings, including the women and children, and the attendance varied greatly from time to time. Some clubs had only about twenty-five or thirty people present at their meetings, while others regularly had an attendance of between two hundred and five hundred. At various times a club might have as many as six hundred attendants, and a few weeks later find its membership reduced to one hundred.

Not all the clubs were open to the public, nor were they all alike in their arrangements. The Club de la Révolution, reviving an electoral distinction which had been temporarily employed during the French Revolution, had two classes of members—active and passive. Only the active members had the right to participate in the election of officers and attend the closed sessions. The requirements for becoming an active member included signing a profession of revolutionary faith and being passed upon by the other members. Some clubs held only secret meetings, and some endeavored to copy the Jacobin clubs of the Great Revolution as much as possible.

In general, the crowds at the clubs were excited but well disciplined. There were no reserved seats, and smoking was allowed. All the meetings closed at 10 o'clock because the gas was extinguished then. At first the clubs sent delegations to the government presenting their demands, but there were so many delegations that the government had to send delegates to speak with the delegates. Then the clubs began to communicate with the government by having the newspapers publish the resolutions or reclamations intended for official ears, rather than having the government treat with the delegations.

It must not be thought that there was unanimity within the clubs; differences of opinion were frequently expressed, although it cannot be said that the audience listened too patiently to an orator who ventured to disagree with the general viewpoint of the auditors. There were frequent arguments as to the best strategy to be used in saving the country and as to the composition of the government. Even when unanimity might be said to have existed among members of a club in regard to their political beliefs they still argued among themselves on various pretexts. Thus, at one of the radical clubs a certain citizen was accused of having been condemned in London for being a thief and of attempting to pose, falsely, as a delegate of the International Workingmen's Association. This citizen defended himself with the coun04charge that another member who pretended to be a former political prisoner had spent three months in a Belgian prison for publication of obscene books. Mutual and violent recriminations filled the air, until a special commission of inquiry was appointed to look into the matter. A similar quarrel arose at the Club Favié on November 10 when a certain citizen, compromised in a bomb plot under the Empire, was accused of having been an *agent provocateur* and spy of the Imperial police, "or at least a drunkard." This citizen was hotly defended by his friends.

On the whole, the clubs provided the people with a chance to "let off steam." They attacked the government, the clergy, the methods of distributing goods, profiteering, and the way in which the military campaign was being run, and they rid themselves of various other antipathies. Not all the clubs were so radical. There were many clubs which were frequented by republicans of moderate views and sympathies, which had serious meetings of their liberal bourgeois membership. At these clubs, the radical tendencies of some of the lower class clubs was deplored. At the Club des Folies-Bérgère, for example, several passages from Blanqui's radical newspaper, *La Patrie en danger,* were booed unanimously when read aloud by a speaker, and the paper was burned on the platform amid great applause. This club, radical in tendency at the beginning of the siege, had gradually become more conservative after the events of October 31, when its members thought the insurrectionists threatened seriously the successful conduct of the siege by their destruction of unity within the city.

But it was the lower-class and radical clubs which provided the most entertaining spectacles and which were to prove politically the most important, for it was there that the dissatisfaction with the government's conduct of the defense was given full vent. Blanqui's club at the Salle de la Rue d'Arras, which name it sometimes took, was notable for the continual denunciations expressed there, as was also the Club de la Reine-Blanche. A typical evening at the latter club included the following denunciations: (1) a woman who fed her four dogs bread; (2) a man who stood in a butcher-shop queue to get food for his dogs and cats; (3) a conductor of the bus company who made an artilleryman of the National Guard pay full fare on the pretense that he did not have his gun with him. "But the gun of the artillery-man," said the orator who brought this abuse to the attention of the audience, "is a cannon; is it necessary then for him to carry his cannon with him to have the right to half-fare?"

Taking the place of regular nocturnal amusements, the clubs sometimes endeavored to present some sort of entertainment, as well as being unconsciously entertaining in what they considered to be their serious moments. The entertainment usually consisted of readings from Victor Hugo's poetry, especially *Les Châtiments,* or from the works of some amateur poet who belonged to the club. In addition, practically every session of the popular clubs was enlivened by the presence of some monomaniac with a sure method for saving Paris, such as poisoning the Seine, loos-ing the wild animals of the zoo on the Prussians, or the use of Greek fire.

The club members saw nothing comical in such schemes. This was an age of science when miracles could be accomplished, and no scheme was too fantastic if it could aid in delivering the city from the Prussians. For, when all was said and done, the important thing to be considered at the club meetings was the defeat of the enemy; all other matters were of secondary consideration or only a prelude to this single overwhelming question. In the meetings, no matter was too trivial, no scheme too harebrained, if it could contribute in some way to final victory. An account of a meeting at the Club de la Chapelle in November serves to il-lustrate this intense preoccupation with the military, and, of

necessity, the political situation of Paris. This club ener-
getically declared that it stood for defense to the last ditch,
and that Paris must refuse a peace, or even an armistice,
just so long as a solitary Prussian remained on French soil.
The government was blamed for its refusal to employ
Greek fire, which the members of the club were convinced
would have a frightening effect upon the enemy, and for not
using any and all means which science could devise for ex-
terminating the invaders. As its final resolution of the evening, the club demanded the replacement of the cautious
government by a commune, a government consisting of the
municipal representatives of Paris, which they felt would
give a more active account of itself in carrying on the war,
just as the defense of France had been carried through by
an earlier communal government during the French Revolution.

Indeed, with the middle of November and the definite
refusal of an armistice, coupled with the reorganization of
the army and the news of the first French victory at Coulmiers, the pressure on the government to adopt an active
policy and the giving of gratuitous military advice reached
new heights. Any means by which the defeat of the Prussians might be accomplished was given a wide hearing in
the clubs and in the newspapers. Although the warfare of
1870 was not mechanized and depersonalized to the extent
of the twentieth-century art of war, great hope was placed
in the work of the scientists who might discover new destructive engines for the purpose of annihilating the Prussians. As soon as the siege had begun, the government had
been flooded with inventions guaranteed to stop the Germans, and the advocacy of these inventions reached a cre-
scendo in the middle of November.

Obviously there were many crackpot schemes suggested,
such as decomposing the air and suffocating the Prussians,

paralyzing them by means of chemical bombs, mobile ramparts, a return to the armor of the Middle Ages, and, especially, Greek fire. The latter had been brought to Paris by two men of Marseilles in the middle of September, and in a short time the patriotic newspapers had all acclaimed it. When some timid souls ventured to speak of humane warfare, Félix Pyat, the fiery republican patriot, proved that it was perfectly all right to use Greek fire against the Prussians who themselves had violated the laws of war. So popular did the idea of Greek fire become that a journal was founded dedicated exclusively to advancing the idea of its employment by the defenders of Paris. This journal, in order to show its unbreakable will to reduce the enemy by any means, also advocated other measures to be used in conjunction with Greek fire, such as letting the Prussians enter Paris and having the women pour boiling oil over them, or having the peasants put germs in the next harvest.

Another invention which achieved great notoriety in the popular clubs and newspapers was Jules Allix's "prussic finger," designed to protect the virtue of Frenchwomen. It consisted of a small tube put on the end of the finger, with a hypodermic needle, almost invisible, protruding from its end. When a Prussian approached, the woman was to prick him with the needle, thereby injecting prussic acid into him and killing him; the patriotic Frenchwoman would thus remain "tranquil and pure, having surrounded herself with a crown of dead men."

An inventor at a meeting of the Club des Folies-Bérgère had an idea for putting Paris in communication with the provinces by means of a series of redoubts in echelon. "One would build the first under the fort of Bicêtre, the second under the cannon of the first, and so on until Etampes, and even farther, if it were necessary." It must be said in behalf of the bourgeois audience of this moderate club that it was skeptical of this plan. But the lower and less well-educated classes were not so skeptical of the many notions advanced before their clubs. The illusion that science could accomplish all never ceased to give them hope that perhaps some one invention might be discovered which would surely and promptly give them victory, or that some marvelous new food might be invented which would save them from starvation and make that victory possible.

Inasmuch as all Paris was putting its mind to the problem of defeating the Prussians, it is no wonder that so many schemes turned up. So great was the flood of inventions guaranteed to stop the Germans that it was necessary for the government to establish a central scientific committee with subcommittees in each arrondissement for the examination of these projects. When the inventors found their ideas rejected by the government, they then turned to the clubs and newspapers to expound them in the hope of getting the political support and public demand which would force the government to try out their respective schemes.

Some of the ideas were ludicrous—for 1870—but they contained the germs of various methods of warfare which were later to be employed at a time when science and civilization had advanced further. And there is humor in some of these ludicrous schemes, if it can be called humorous to plan the death of one's fellow men even by an utterly impracticable scheme. One inventor, for example, disclaimed the title of inventor for himself, stating that he merely adapted the lessons of ancient history to the circumstances of Paris in 1870. As a result, he believed that he had an idea which was a modification of the Trojan horse theme. It involved sending one army of 25,000 men to attack the enemy positions to the north of Paris, and another of 50,000 men to the south of Paris, both of these armies to be perfectly visible to the Germans inasmuch as they were to begin their attacks before dusk. Under cover of darkness, however, the main body of 150,000 men, screened and entirely concealed by a movable wall of sheet iron blackened by smoke, was to advance in still a third direction. While the Prussians were diverted in the direction of the two feinting attacks, the third army, protected and made invisible by the blackened sheet iron, could penetrate the Prussian lines unhindered, thereby causing a panic among the Germans who would not know whence the enemy came since they could not see the sheet-iron wall in the darkness.

Another inventor had something no less formidable in mind. His idea was to have a giant sledge hammer, fifteen miles in circumference and weighing ten million tons, lifted up to a certain altitude by balloons and sent in the direction of Versailles where the ropes confining the hammer could be cut. In its fall it would crush and bury the headquarters and bulk of the German army. Still another inventor revealed some insight into what later came to be known as psychological warfare. His scheme involved a "musical *mitrailleuse*" which would spray the enemy with machine-gun bullets while playing Wagner, Schubert, and Mendelssohn. According to this inventor, "The Germans are too fond of music to be able to resist the temptation of listening. They are sure to draw near in thousands when my machine guns are playing. We have got them at our mercy."

The government listened politely to all such schemes, but it preferred to put its trust in the professional scientists rather than the amateur inventors and armchair strategists. And the men of science responded to the government's call. Many investigations were carried on by competent scientists, and some of these were fruitful, especially in the realm of aerial navigation, antiseptics, gunpowder, and rapid-firing guns. Even the staid academicians took cogni-

zance of the military situation. At the Academy of Science
the meetings presented a mixture of its regular scientific
activities and new activities forced upon it by the conditions of the siege. For example, the meeting of September 28 was the occasion of discourses on the provisioning
of a besieged town, the aurora borealis, and the cerebral
forms of mammals. On October 24 the attention of the
scientists was turned to such varied subjects as the coming
eclipse of the sun, the relations of physical astronomy with
geology, a new foodstuff called *bouilli romaine,* the effects
of bouillon made with beef blood, and balloons and aerial
navigation. Spectroanalysis and artillery were the two main
topics at the meeting of November 7.

The chemists, of course, worked hard on the question
of preserving the available food supply in good condition and on creating new artificial gastronomic substances.
Osseine, a new gelatinous food preparation invented by
Frémy, was the chief topic of discussion at the session of
November 28, but that meeting also included an address
on differential linear equations, a talk on a method for
destroying compromising papers rapidly in case a balloon
should be captured by the enemy, and a discussion of
meteors. In addition to serving as a scientific testing-ground
for new ideas connected with the siege, the Academy of
Sciences was also the scene of many patriotic discourses and
protests in which the Germans were held to be barbarians
and condemned for their destruction of the treasures of
science, art, and letters contained in the besieged towns of
France.

The Academy of Inscriptions and Letters was, of course,
not so influenced by the siege as was the scientific Academy.
It continued to hold its regular meetings and discussed its
usual topics, such as medieval grammar, ancient Egyptian
history, and Coptic inscriptions. This Academy was also

interested in taking precautions in regard to rare books and manuscripts which might be damaged by bombardment, and it did take some notice of the siege in November by a talk on "The Provisioning of Besieged Towns in Antiquity."

Even the realms of so-called "pure thought" were invaded. Thus the sessions of the Academy of Moral and Political Sciences reveal the influence of the war and the siege, even though the agenda of its programs continued to contain topics discussed in more normal times, such as Buddhist morality and "Economic and Financial Reform in England since 1842." But the impact of the war on the minds of the French philosophers was shown in the two sessions devoted entirely to Hegel and his philosophy. The reports of these meetings indicate how even the Olympian philosophers were affected by what Francis Bacon might have termed the "Idols of the Battlefield." M. Beausire, for example, delivered an address which showed that King William and Bismarck were, after all, only disciples of Hegel, and M. Wolowski agreed with this interpretation by protesting against the cult of brute force contained in the Hegelian doctrine. Only M. Barthélemy-Saint-Hilaire evidenced some of that calm which we expect from thinkers on philosophical problems by stating that he felt a certain respect for Hegel and especially for his philosophy of history, and that the time was unfavorable for an impartial judgment regarding Hegel, nor should the German philosopher be held responsible for the aberrations of his strange disciples. However, the general opinion of the meeting did not seem to favor this restrained judgment, and, as the reporter of the session remarked, "After all, a tree is known by its fruits. . . . The material result of Hegelianism is the wicked and barbarous war which destroys us. . . . As for the arguments of the militant disciples of Hegel, there is, according to the vigorous expression of General Trochu, only one answer to make: fight!"

Indeed, by the end of November Trochu was ready, to some extent at least, to attempt to make good his fighting words and promises to the people. The time was certainly ripe, if not overripe. Possibilities for an armistice were dead, at least temporarily, and there existed a victorious army in the field, with the prospect of others to come and aid in the rescue of beleaguered Paris. The populace was anxious for some military action, because, with the exception of the battle at le Bourget, the failure of which had helped touch off the incidents of October 31, there had been no large-scale attempt to break the investing circle. In addition, the defending forces had just undergone a reorganization which increased their fighting power somewhat. Finally, there was little to be hoped for in further delay, and Gambetta was insistent that the defenders of Paris make some effort to break out of the circle and join the armies of the provinces. The pressure of a "second front" from the inside of Paris to aid the armies engaged in fighting the Germans outside the city was so great that it could not be denied.

The plan was for Paladines with his Army of the Loire to drive to the north from the direction of Orleans, while the defenders of Paris were to attempt a great sortie to the south with the hope of breaking through the investing lines and meeting the army of Paladines. The Germans would be caught between these two armies and would be unable to cope with this dual attack. Gambetta expected great things from this plan, and he had sent carrier pigeons to Trochu in Paris saying that Paladines would make his attack and that November 28 would be the day when the guns of Paladines' army could be heard in Paris; then Trochu was to make his sortie and meet the Army of the

Loire. Trochu's plans called for the National Guard under General Clément Thomas to hold the city while General Vinoy's army made a feinting attack in the directions of east, west, and north. The big attack was to be under the direction of General Ducrot, who was to lead his army, consisting of the best fighting men which Paris contained, to the south, in an attempt to pierce the Prussian lines and meet the troops of Paladines.

Before this great sortie took place, Ducrot endeavored to inflame his troops by a proclamation exhorting them to think of honor, liberty, and country. If that motive did not suffice, he also reminded them of the devastation wrought by the enemy and of their sisters, wives, and mothers. Finally, he swore to re-enter Paris "either dead or victorious," but not to retreat. Trochu also issued a proclamation, somewhat less flamboyant in tone, but the whole spirit of the city was aroused by the expectation of some genuine military action at last.

Indeed, this great sortie represented the most serious attempt that had yet been made, or that was to be made, to break out of Paris, as von Moltke himself admitted. There was every prospect for success, if that were possible, because the great attempt was to be made at what was the weakest point in the investing circle at that moment. Furthermore, the attempt was on the largest scale yet tried, and there was the hope of assistance from the armies of Paladines coming from the south.

But what Trochu and the Parisians did not realize was that even at the moment that they started their great sortie, the hoped-for assistance from the armies outside Paris would not materialize. On November 28, Paladines, instead of breaking the German lines on the plain of Beauce, stretching between Orleans and Toury, had himself been defeated, and the Army of the Loire was being driven back into the entrenched camps of Orleans. Meanwhile the sortie from Paris started out with initial success. Ducrot's army succeeded in crossing the Marne and fighting a bloody battle at Champigny. But the Germans rallied, retook the positions which they had lost temporarily, and on December 3 succeeded in forcing Ducrot back across the Marne to Vincennes. This great attempt to break the siege, which the people had watched with bated breath from the heights of the city, had failed. The disappointment and despair were made more acute by the fact that the government had given forth encouraging news at first and had raised the Parisians' hopes very high.

And, despite his high-sounding words, General Ducrot had returned—neither dead nor victorious.

Chapter IV

Escape . . . into Reality

After this unsuccessful sortie, the period of inaction began again, while Paris recovered from its wounds, both physical and psychical. Indeed, the last was quite a problem, because after the high hopes for the deliverance of Paris by the sortie at the end of November, there had been an inevitable reaction which was depressing to the populace. The newness and excitement of life in a besieged town were giving way to boredom, especially when it was seen that prospects for a successful culmination of the siege had been dimmed somewhat.

Enough news trickled in to give the Parisians fresh material for conversation and thought every now and then, but this did not prevent them from being taken with boredom in their daily life. To the cosmopolitan residents of the capital, the depressing effects of the last sortie made life in Paris similar to the ennui of a town in the provinces. Just as the monotony of military life eventually affects every soldier, so the Parisians, leading a collective military life in a besieged city, began to feel the monotony of war.

It had taken some time for the Parisians to begin to feel bored. At the time of the arrival of the enemy before the city, the excitement of Parisian daily life had not been lessened, nor did the first fortnight of the siege witness any notable change in that respect. But as the siege wore on and certain restrictive military regulations were put into effect, the daily life of Paris had begun to take on a routine cast after the first thrilling moments of military preparation.

Life in the besieged capital began to be stereotyped. Every morning Paris was awakened at 7 o'clock by the sound of cannon and drums and the shouts of the newsboys. From nine until noon the inhabitants read the newspapers, gossiped, and spent a great deal of time in food queues. At noon there was a lull in the day's inactivity, followed by drilling in the afternoon and general promenading by the citizenry when weather permitted. The evenings were scarcely more exciting, although at 7:00 P.M. there was a slight flurry around the kiosks formed by people waiting for the evening newspapers to appear.

Paris was ordinarily a capital of late hours, but the police regulations and the diminution in the supply of illuminating gas constrained the Parisians to eat quickly and go to bed early. Every shop and café closed at 10:30 P.M. in order to remove temptation from the way of the soldiers from the provinces, and shortly thereafter the streets were deserted, the clubs usually having finished their meetings by that time also. In November the closing hours of the cafés had been extended to midnight, but this did not mean any increase in the night life of the majority of the citizens. They still found it desirable to go to sleep earlier and to awaken later because that mitigated somewhat the effects of the hunger and cold.

To relieve the boredom, many Parisians formed the habit of walking around the city inspecting the fortifications. This was especially the case on Sunday afternoons, inasmuch as the Parisians were unable to take their regular promenade in the Bois de Vincennes or the Bois de

Boulogne. Some people got a thrill, albeit a vicarious one, by going to the viaduct of Auteuil or to the heights of the Trocadéro and watching the Prussians, or looking through the telescopes at the forts of Issy and Meudon, or silently admiring Mont Valérien, considered to be the strongest fort protecting Paris. Refugees from the suburbs often went to the heights to see how their beloved property was faring, seeming to derive some consolation from a glance at it.

The Parisians spent a large part of their time in listening to orators, watching military reviews, sending deputations to the City Hall, searching for spies, and discussing the news. "Each National Guardsman thought himself to be a transcendent military genius; and in this capacity he considered he possessed a perfect right to criticize in detail every arrangement that was made." This despite the fact that the men of the Guard were thought so ignorant about arms that there were frequent items in the daily newspapers giving them advice on how to aim their guns, a sad commentary on the amount of training which the military officials had seen fit to give these citizen soldiers. It was left to the newspapers also, rather than to any formal training, to inform the National Guard how to recognize the uniforms of the different corps of the German army, since they had acquired the distressing habit of firing on French soldiers, mistaking them for Prussians.

As always, the Parisian boulevards were crowded on Sundays, but this was especially true on the rare sunny days. Circulation on the streets was virtually impossible on such days because of the number of hawkers who had set up stands. Nevertheless, these weekly walks helped provide some temporary relief from the ennui.

The people who attempted to go about their ordinary business during the siege were also taken with boredom.

Many of the workers had been thrown out of work by the shutting down of their ordinary places of business. The proprietors of stores still kept them open, but there was very little business. It was the heyday of window shopping, but the people rarely bought anything. All that could be done was to sit around and discuss the military and political situations and hope that something could be done about them.

The search for excitement in the periods of inaction between the military engagements brought many people to attend the sending off of balloons to the provinces. Until the balloons began to be dispatched too early in the morning, the Parisians had satisfied their curiosity, and also relieved the tediousness of their daily existence, by seeing the balloons off. It was also considered fashionable to be weighed once a week and see how many pounds one had lost on his siege diet.

The boredom was forgotten when an important military engagement was going on outside the city; then the Parisians crowded around the gates of the capital, waiting for news of the results of the sortie or scanning with apprehension the faces of the occupants of the ambulance vans. But the periods of action were few and far between, and most of the time the Parisians were bored, once the novelty of their situation had worn off.

It would have been impossible for the Parisians, thoroughly imbued with the gay and frivolous spirit fostered by the Empire, to continue for any great length of time to concentrate their thoughts and energies upon the siege and its problems and to lead a life of boredom and monotony without any letup or attempt to ease the tension. For this reason, amusements unconnected with the situation in which the Parisians found themselves gradually came back into the scene whence they had fled with the Revolution of September 4. The alternation of periods of intense excitement during military operations with longer periods of inactivity made some sort of amusement necessary. After all, even the excitement was repetitious, because it ended always with the same result—defeat, despair, and fatigue.

But—and here again we come into contact with the thorough manner in which the siege was all-pervasive in the Parisian life—even the amusements and cultural activities designed to divert the minds of the citizens from their plight could not help being connected in many ways with the current circumstances. Even the august Academies had turned their attention to matters dealing with the siege. In the same way, art, literature, the theater, and any one of the many activities into which the people might throw themselves to be relieved of the tediousness or excitement of daily existence reflected the very facts from which the people sought escape.

The activities of the theaters in Paris during the siege provide proof of this. Most of them had closed after September 4. It was felt that theater performances of the light and frothy type which had been typical of the Second Empire were out of tune with the general atmosphere of the time. Besides, theatrical receipts had declined because everybody was interested in military preparations, and many of the theatrical troupes had melted away, some of the actors leaving Paris for the safety of the provinces before the siege set in, and others staying to perform patriotic duties as nurses or soldiers. Furthermore, the press of military necessity had brought about the conversion of many theaters into hospitals, barracks, etc.

This condition could not last for long when it became evident that amusements of some kind were necessary. Gradually the theaters began to reopen for benefit performances, the Théâtre-Français taking the lead on October 25 with a performance featured by scenes from *Horace* and the *Misanthrope,* and a talk by Edmund Legouvé on "Moral Food during the Siege." During the month of November, the Comédie-Française instituted successful weekly performances, characterized by the recital of "works of the times"—*pièces de circonstance*—between the acts, dealing with various episodes of the war, such as Coppée's "Letters of a Breton Mobile Guard" and Bergerat's patriotic "Cuirassiers of Reichshoffen." By far the most successful of the poetry readings was Victor Hugo's *Les Châtiments,* extracts from which were given on practically every occasion, and which by the middle of December had sold 22,000 copies in Paris. Hugo was *persona grata* now that the Empire had been overthrown. In addition, the theater censorship which had been unfavorable to his works had been abolished by the Ministry of Public Instruction of the new regime.

But these theatrical performances did not perform the task of taking the minds of the Parisians away from their daily troubles by emphasizing the lighter aspects of life. Indeed, the Comédie-Française in its performances made the people even more conscious of their troubles by performing classical works without costumes, and, on the whole, the presentations of the great theaters were characterized by lugubriousness and sadness, which hardly provided an escape at all. The Ambigu-Comique was the first theater to reopen avowedly for the purpose of entertaining rather than instructing the public. Despite the success of this theater and of other theaters which followed its lead, the performances—light as well as heavy—soon encountered an insurmountable obstacle in the lack of fuel, which made it impossible to heat the theaters as the weather became colder in December. Although the audience sat in furs and wraps, the cold became so bitter that performances had ceased by the end of December, with the sole exception of a celebration of the 244th anniversary of the birth of Molière at the Théâtre-Français on January 15.

Music underwent the same cyclical behavior as did the drama. Here, too, performances had been discontinued after September 4, and when they were renewed they were more serious than the music popularized by the Second Empire, when Offenbach, Auber, and Halévy had been the music masters. As in the case of the theater, concerts were given for benefits for the Red Cross and other purposes. The Opéra also reopened in November with a benefit performance. Naturally, all concerts and operas closed at an early hour in order to economize on lighting.

A singular fact must be noted in connection with music during the siege: that is the popularity of the works of "those Prussians"—Mendelssohn, Meyerbeer, Weber, and Beethoven. However, as the music critics were careful to point out, these men belonged to "the country of genius" and had nothing in common with the army at the gates of Paris or "with the barbarous race struggling . . . against civilization." Music, just as the theater, eventually met the invincible obstacle of fuel, and concert and operatic performances were gradually suspended as the weather grew more and more severe.

In the field of fine arts, there was very little activity during the siege, except in the museums where feverish preparations were made to protect the treasures within from bombardment and fire. Although Cézanne, and perhaps others, shirked their patriotic duties, the artists as a whole were not slack in serving their country. Many of the Parisian artists served in the Artists' Battalion of the National Guard, with Meissonier as colonel, while others devoted themselves to various types of defense work.

Some of the artists used their spare time while on guard

duty in compiling sketches which were later used in their paintings, while Meissonier's unit took time off to build snow sculptures in the middle of December. The artists were also active in war relief work, and all of them responded generously to an appeal for gifts for a benefit exhibition held in the foyer of the Opéra.

Gustave Courbet, later to play an important role in the Commune, headed the "Artistic Commission for the Preservation of National Museums and Objects of Art." In this post he had already conceived the plan which was to bear fruit during the civil strife which followed the siege, namely, "the destruction of the Vendôme column, as having no artistic value, and tending to perpetuate ideas of war and conquest and the memory of the Imperial dynasty." Courbet's commission for the "preservation of national museums and objects of art" evidently did not interfere with his political program of destroying any reminders of the Napoleonic regime.

It is in the field of caricature rather than of painting and sculpture that the siege is especially fecund, but even here the work was not escapist in nature. The caricatures dealt mainly with political and military events of the day, although much of their political comment was seasoned with a goodly amount of obscenity and pornography. But the amusement provided by these drawings, most of which were published on separate sheets and hung up before the kiosks and magazine sellers, was not sufficient to divert the Parisians from their constant preoccupation with the siege.

With business at a standstill and many of the workers unemployed, it might be expected that the Parisians would use some of their new-found leisure time in reading, especially since the cabarets, theaters, and other peacetime amusements were closed, or, at best, only intermittent in their performances. With this end in view, Jules Simon, the Minister of Public Instruction, had increased the number of hours during which the reading rooms of the public libraries would remain open. Furthermore, many libraries closed to the public under the Empire were now made accessible. Despite these increased facilities offered by the government, not many people seemed interested in profiting by these reforms during the siege.

The clubs, of course, provided a place of amusement, but their constant preoccupation with military and political problems, as we have seen, would hardly make them a place of escape from the issues of the day. Indeed, during the month of December, the clubs suffered a temporary eclipse, a decline in popularity, owing perhaps to the heating problem which had conquered the efforts of the theaters and concerts and perhaps also to the need for something far removed from activities connected with the siege.

If the Parisians were thus unable to find an escape from the siege in intellectual activities, perhaps we should look to physical activities for some measure of escape. Here again the influence of the siege was inevitable. The closing years of the Empire had brought with them a great interest in horse racing, skating, and cycling. There was no racing during the siege, horses being more useful to line men's stomachs than their pocketbooks, and skating and cycling appear to have suffered a temporary decline.

Nevertheless, the sporting instinct was not dormant in this winter of 1870–1871, and it was fortified in some respects by the absence of food and by the military situation. Thus we find that fishing in the Seine was a utilitarian as well as sporting endeavor, and when the weather became too cold to allow such activity, the disciples of Izaak Walton fell back on fishing for rats in the sewers. And it was always open season for bird hunting during the siege, except, of course, for pigeons.

With the leisure time afforded them by the monotonous guard duty of the ramparts, the National Guard, when they were not engaged in drinking or in comradely argument, were participating in various sports such as pitch-and-toss and bowling. The military situation gave added impetus to another sport. The shooting galleries, especially those on the Boulevard St. Michel, were the scenes of nightly queues, where the ambitious marksmen took turns in improving their aim and compensated for the lack of Prussians at which to shoot by firing at inanimate targets.

Naturally enough, certain avenues of escape took the form of vice. Although the Revolutionary tradition in France called for a "Republic of Virtue," the newly founded Third Republic found it no easier than its predecessors to obliterate certain common human failings. Gambling, for example, continued unabated during the siege. The National Guard spent a large portion of their time, even while on duty at the ramparts, in playing dice and other games of chance. Nor was gambling confined to the lower classes. It had been a popular pastime among the upper classes during the Empire, and, with the other means of amusement cut down during the siege, there is reason to believe that those classes spent as much, if not more, time at the gaming table during this period than before.

One form of gambling ever popular in France is lotteries, but these were forbidden during the siege. Only one lottery was held—for the benefit of the wounded—and it was allowed because during the early days of the Republic a mistaken authorization had been granted for this lottery, but others were forbidden thereafter.

The siege, of course, was not lacking in purely physical

avenues of escape. The ancient connection between Mars and Venus was certainly not broken by the proclamation of the Republic or by the siege, and it was probably augmented by the famine which undoubtedly drove many women into prostitution. Despite the fact that certain ardent republicans had stated that prostitution could not exist in the Republic, it did exist during the siege, but the amount of it, or rather its conspicuousness, seems to have varied at different times.

Near the beginning of the siege, during the first flush of revolutionary and republican enthusiasm, the police had organized a dragnet which had attempted to sweep Paris clean of all the underworld elements, including the prostitutes. But this was only a temporary matter. Some observers claimed that the prostitutes were more aggressive during the siege than before, while others found them more retiring than before. Inasmuch as such comments might be merely a reflection of the tastes of the contemporary observers, it is difficult, if not impossible, to judge of the behavior of the prostitutes at this time. However, if Zola's picture of a prostitute, Nana, under the Second Empire is accepted as a true portrait, it is hard to imagine the prostitutes as becoming more aggressive or more insolently conspicuous than they had been before.

Perhaps the presence of the professional prostitutes was not felt so much within the city during the siege because many of them made their headquarters in the surrounding suburbs which were occupied by troops of the Mobile Guard. Although the soldiers had special prostitutes, the presence of any large body of men was bound to attract others. Certainly the presence of 8,000 venereal cases in the Paris garrison shows how widespread prostitution must have been.

The Siege of Paris

On January 1, 1870, there had been 152 whore houses in Paris, but this number was down to 133 by the end of the year. However, this decrease does not necessarily indicate a decrease in the amount of illicit love for sale, for not all the prostitution carried on within Paris seems to have been done by professional whores. Living conditions being what they were, it would not be surprising if some women should have been driven to sell their bodies just so they could have enough to eat. One of the omnipresent Goncourt brothers recorded such an incident during the siege: "A girl, walking up behind me in the rue Saint-Nicholas, throws in my ear, '*Monsieur, voulez-vous monter chez moi . . . pour un morceau de pain?*' "

Perhaps the pleasure of alcohol provided a less temporary form of escape than did that of prostitution, for drinking was one social evil which was definitely increased by the siege. Wine was never lacking during the siege, and it was still fairly cheap, so many people made up for the absence of solids in their diet by extensive drinking. Despite this, there were few drunken brawls on the streets, probably because of the National Guard patrols, although these citizen soldiers were not blameless themselves in the matter of drink.

Indeed, the armed forces took the lead when it came to drunkenness. It was not an uncommon sight for men to be on duty while under the influence of liquor, and the marching qualities of the National Guard, which was never well trained, sometimes suffered from the inability of its members to walk in a straight line, let alone keep in step with their neighbors. Even the provincial Mobiles, whose morale and morals seem to have been weakened by contact with Paris, succumbed to the vice of alcoholism, so that General Ducrot was led to state that "drunkenness and debauchery caused almost as much damage in their ranks as the fire of the enemy." [1] The government was almost powerless to cope with this increase in drinking, although it did forbid the serving of the more insidious poisons, such as absinthe, in the canteens on the ramparts.

But we should not be misled into thinking that the Parisians or their defenders walked around in a continual alcoholic stupor. There are several extenuating factors: most of the drinking was done on empty stomachs, and the quality of the liquor consumed was not of the highest. And, although the drinking in Paris increased in relation to that before the war, it was still probably not so great as that in other large cities of Europe. Alcoholism had not yet become a major social problem in France. And inasmuch as alcohol can be a depressive as well as a stimulant, it is not likely that the escape to be found in drink could be achieved successfully unless one chose to drink oneself into a state of complete insensibility.

While there were many who sought escape from the siege by an abandonment to physical pleasures, there were others who thought to find relief through religion. Although times of stress frequently turn people's thoughts toward religion, the extent is impossible of measurement. Even if we were to consider attendance figures at the churches as an index of the amount of religious interest—an unwarranted assumption—we should still be unable to measure any changes in religious interest during the siege because of the complete absence of figures in that respect. Also, many of the churches had been forced to close their doors because of the impossibility of heating and lighting the buildings, and so many of the Protestant foreigners had left Paris that the Protestant ministers could have conducted their services in their vestry rooms without any

---

[1] General A. A. Ducrot, *La Défense de Paris* (2d ed.; Paris, 1876–1878), I, 89.

crowding. One factor which might conceivably have increased church attendance was the presence of battalions from the provinces within Paris, especially the Breton Mobile Guard, which had a reputation for piety.

Even if we could find out if and how church attendance varied during the siege, we would still be unable to determine whether the siege conditions made for more or less religiosity. Despite the services rendered by the clergy during the siege and the crusades of the ultramontanes against the unbelievers, the seeds sown at the time of the siege by the traditionally anticlerical republicanism and radicalism of Paris were to be reaped in the Commune. Evidently religion provided no more of an escape to the bulk of the population than did gambling or drinking.

If drama, art, music, religion, vice could provide no escape for the Parisians from the siege, what other opportunities were open for them? How could they find some relief, some surcease, from the depressing military and political situation and the accompanying hunger and freezing which oppressed them? The answer is that there was no escape from the actuality of the siege. No matter in what direction the Parisians turned, they could not help being reminded of their situation. Their eyes, ears, and nostrils were assailed continually by the sights, sounds, and smells of a city at war. Any intellectual, physical, or moral relief which they might seek proved in the end to be affected in some way by the conditions of the siege. The minds and emotions of the Parisians could no more escape from the encircled city than could their bodies.

Any cataclysmic event exercises a profound influence upon the psychology of a nation, and this is especially the case with the siege of Paris. This was so not only because of the extraordinary situation which the siege produced and the length of time the people were subjected to certain stimuli, but also because of the changes engendered in the Parisian "emotional climate" during the course of the war and siege. It is no wonder that the Parisians could not find an avenue of escape which would free them from their problems, because the psychical atmosphere itself would not have admitted of such escape. It is all very well for Arnold Bennett, not having been in Paris during this time, to write a novel, *The Old Wives' Tale*, wherein the siege has practically no effect upon the characters who lived through it, but the inhabitants of Paris during the siege felt its effects in their stomachs, hearts, and minds.

How could it be otherwise when the Parisians found themselves living within sound of cannon fire, having a steadily diminishing food supply, and constantly subjected to uncertainty and fear? That nerve-wracking uncertainty and fear were increased by the privation of news and the lack of contact with the outside world, and by the boredom of men willing and anxious to fight but rarely given the opportunity to do so. Paris had become an enlarged prison for a population of over two million people.

The nervous excitement precipitated by the situation of Paris was bound to have a great effect upon minds that had a predisposition to the psychotic. It might be expected that in France such events would give rise to many imitators of Joan of Arc, and that was actually the case. One of them, Amélie Seulart, even went so far as to sign her manifestoes "Joan of Arc II." One of the period's experts in mental diseases informs us—somewhat unnecessarily—that all the Joans of Arc who suddenly appeared in 1870 were simple lunatics to whom the siege merely gave a new opportunity for expression. Collective madness among the women was manifested by the group called the "Amazons of the Seine."

Another form of psychosis was, however, peculiarly absent from the siege. Suicides were extremely rare, the Prefecture of Police reporting only five deaths by suicide during the whole period. Perhaps the nervous excitement engendered during the siege was not conducive to this type of psychotic behavior. The optimism and credulity of the early period of the siege might also have acted to mitigate too great despair. Even the worst news could not conquer the optimism and confidence of the Parisians. One reason which might be advanced to explain the sanguineness of Parisians—with the exception of their conservative military leaders who did not share their hopes—was their self-consciousness of their own courage. They were continually complimenting themselves in that respect.

When the flood of bad news had become a deluge, the Parisians made up for it by welcoming doubly any ray of sunshine which shone upon their cause. The announcement of the retaking of Orleans by the troops of General Paladines had created an immense sensation. At the news of the risings in the provinces, the elastic Parisian spirit stretched to the heights of exaltation. But when the news of the defeat of the Army of the Loire came, and when Orleans was recaptured by the Germans during the first week in December, the Parisians did not relapse into the depths of despair. Instead, they refused at first to believe in the truth of such bad news, and, when finally convinced, still did not feel that irreparable harm had been done to their cause.

The truth about the matter is that Paris was completely taken in by its own illusions and hopes of victory. Despite repeated and bitter disillusionments, the Parisian masses remained optimistic to the end. Angered at the beginning of the war by the failure of other countries to assist her, Paris was hopeful throughout the siege for the mediation of neutral countries, such as Russia and the United States. Faced by continual failures on the battlefield, the citizens retained their confidence and belief in ultimate victory.

A veritable "will to believe" was displayed by the Parisians in their desire to accept unquestionably any news or interpretation thereof, true or false, which might be construed as indicative of Prussian weakness or an ultimate French victory. In the first week of December there was a rumor, eagerly seized upon by the besieged, of the complete capture of the Prussian fleet, although actually the fates of the fleets would not have had any decisive effect upon the outcome of the war anyhow.

Nor did the check suffered by the sortie toward the Marne at the end of November dampen the Parisian spirit as much as it should have, for they did not consider it an irreparable loss. One of the George Fielding Eliots of the day even stated that this showed that the plans of the French were first beginning to be executed, while those of von Moltke no longer existed (!). Hence von Moltke would have to improvise others, which, of course, the Prussians were unable to do as well as the French. Evidently Sedan had not yet taught the French officer corps anything about the dangers of improvisation.

A similar compulsion to turn bad news into good can be seen in the matter of the taking of the town of Orleans. The recapture of Orleans by the French in November had been hailed as presaging imminent victory for France, but the recapture of the same town by the Germans a month later was now, by a curious twist of logic, interpreted as pointing to a possible collapse within Germany. Von Moltke had seen fit to send a note to Trochu informing him that the Germans had retaken Orleans, and the Parisian pundits had immediately converted this note into a symptom of German weakness: "Does not the haste of the Prussians in letting us know so quickly of the retaking of Orleans by their army betray a secret anxiety on their side, and perhaps a terrible crisis? Who knows that they are not more pressed outside than we inside? Who knows that they have not much more need than we have of finishing it?" [2]

One thing must be said in behalf of the Parisians and their unwarranted confidence: not all the optimism was generated within the city itself. One of the few sources of news from the outside was the dispatches sent from the provinces by Gambetta, and these were invariably rosy-hued and overly optimistic. Besides painting too bright a picture, the Parisian military leaders, after the war was over, claimed that Gambetta's letters caused the government to carry on the defense in the wrong way and to take part in actions which were of no strategical utility, such as the bloody sortie of the Marne. When it was all over and too late, the army chiefs claimed that they had thought out better plans but they were forced to abandon them because of Gambetta's pressure for an attack toward the Marne. Only one thing causes us to doubt the words of these generals: their plans for victory, which they published in great detail after the war was over and lost, were never mentioned while the siege was going on. Trochu claimed to have a "plan," but, instead of bringing it to the attention of his colleagues in the government, he had deposited it with his lawyer, M. Ducloup. When opened later, it was discovered that this document "was a testament wherein the legacies were replaced by interminable tirades (against his colleagues) and wherein there was not a word of a project of any sort."

However, there is a germ of truth in the complaints of the generals, for the paucity of communications with the outside world made it extremely difficult to acquire any information concerning the disposition and strength of the enemy as well as of one's own forces—both of which items

---

[2] (Emile Chevalet), *Mon journal pendant le siège et la Commune par un bourgeois de Paris* (Paris, 1871), p. 178.

are necessary for effective military planning. But the military leaders were not the only ones who felt the pinch of news. It was inevitable that the Parisians spend a good deal of their time in reading and discussing the news and the situation in which they found themselves, a practice which seemed to bloom all the more because of the very dearth of material to nourish it. The anxiety for news weighed heavily on the population.

To cater to this craze for news, intensified by the difficulties in procuring it, a multitude of new journals and newspapers had come into being after September 4. This sudden growth in the number of publications was the result of another factor: they were now freed from the strangling grip of the Empire. Despite its later and more liberal press laws, the Imperial regime had still required a large money deposit as security for press offenses and had also imposed the *timbre,* a kind of stamp tax, on publications. The Revolution of September 4 had done away with these irksome financial responsibilities as well as the threat of censorship.

The Parisian newspapers during the siege represented every kind of political opinion, the most famous perhaps being those of the extreme radical republicans, led by *La Patrie en danger* of Blanqui, *Le Combat* edited by Félix Pyat, and Délescluze's *Le Réveil.* Almost all of these leftist newspapers had adopted the French Revolutionary calendar on their masthead as a sign that they claimed to be the heirs of the tradition of the Great Revolution. In addition to the radical papers, there were the conservative journals, distinguished by able and serious editing. The two chief examples of this type were the *Journal des Débats* and *Le Temps.* A third class of journals may be discerned: the sensational and "yellow" newspapers, evidently influenced by the *littérature à l'américaine.* These papers fed the Parisians on flattery, chauvinism, and hopeful but false news.

Besides these three main types of newspapers in Paris during the siege, there were many specialized journals instituted for special purposes. Thus we have newspapers dedicated to the plebiscite and to the advocacy of Greek fire; journals published for the benefit of the suburban refugees in Paris; a paper designed to promote Russian interests in France; and a weekly dedicated to the rights and interests of women. Somewhat startling at a time when railway operation was thrown out of joint by the invasion and when manufacturing and trade were either stagnating or struggling under abnormal conditions was the appearance in the midst of the siege of a new *Review of Railroads, Credit, Commerce and Industry*. Obviously there were some people who had faith in the economic recovery of France.

The desire of the Parisians to send news to the provinces gave rise to some inventions which combined letter writing with newspapers, and which were dispatched from Paris by balloon. First among such was the *Lettre-Journal* of D. Jouast, printed on small, light letter paper and having a concise summary of the news on two sides plus space for a short message. The success of this initial venture led to a host of imitations, and microscopic editions of newspapers, obtained by photography, and for the purpose of corresponding with the provinces, soon made their appearance. The *Débats* did not succumb to this combination newspaper-letter fad but ran off special thin-paper copies to be sent to the provinces.

News from the outside was extremely difficult to obtain, and consequently the Paris papers reprinted the news from foreign papers which were two or more weeks old. Whenever any provincial or foreign newspapers succeeded

in reaching Paris, the news contained therein was repro-
duced and commented upon in detail. Frequently the
Parisians were without news from the outside world for
more than a week, and twice during the siege they remained ignorant of events outside Paris for at least twenty
days. The anxiety caused by such lack of contact with the
rest of the world was relieved only by finding copies of
German papers on war prisoners, by chancing on some
stray copies of Bismarck's *Moniteur,* published at the German headquarters in Versailles, or by discovering a few
pages of the Cologne *Zeitung* wrapped around sausages in
the pockets of Rhinelanders killed on the battlefields before Paris. By publishing a special supplement consisting
of an exact facsimile (complete with French translation) of
the Leipzig *Daheim* of December 10, *Le Figaro,* more than
two weeks later, was able to "scoop" its rivals.

Perhaps it was the difficulty of procuring news from
the outside that led to the fabrication of false news—a practice which was all the more serious because of the gulli-
bility of the public and its willingness to believe anything
hopeful. Or perhaps it was just a case of "jumpy nerves"
which enabled reports, such as that in *Le Français* of December 15, to gain credence, whereby, on the basis of a few
shots having been heard from the direction of Versailles,
the rumor was bruited about that the provincial armies
were at last coming to the rescue of Paris.

The dissemination of false news was made easier because the government, like its Imperial predecessor, endeavored to withhold bad news. Actually, the government
need not have withheld such news, because public opinion
was so conditioned that it held bad news to be false news.
The *Débats,* for example, had blamed a Prussian plot to
undermine Parisian morale for the article of *Le Combat*
prematurely announcing the capitulation of Metz, while the

Journal officiel vehemently denied the veracity of the report. The government committed other imbecilities in regard to news. It suspended *La Patrie* for several days near the end of December for revealing the military information that a sortie was to be attempted, when the government itself had already advertised the action by posting signs to the effect that the gates of the city would be closed on a certain day in view of the projected military action. Furthermore, the government had earlier allowed all the newspapers to print detailed stories of the status of the military preparations of Paris and what remained to be done, thereby providing the Prussians with exact knowledge of the extent and readiness of the Parisian defenses.

That the problem of false news was not a trifling one may be seen in an official decree which prohibited newspaper venders from shouting out the news, since they misled the public. But even though the newsboys could not shout out false news, that did not prevent the papers from publishing it. Rumors were magnified and inflated, and so we find reports on the death of General von der Thann and the wounding of Prince Frederick Charles of the German forces, or that the Gladstone Cabinet in England had been overthrown and a war ministry formed in preparation for combat with Prussia, or various "inside stories" on the starvation and suffering within Germany which would surely make Bismarck sue for peace in a short time.

Lack of news from the outside did not serve to subdue the Parisian press so much as the fact that the paper stock began to run low, since no new supplies could enter the city. In December the journals began to be printed on thinner or coarser paper, with an altered format, and sometimes with their regular four pages cut to two. Galignani's *Messenger,* an English-language newspaper, had suspended publication in September; its news sources had dried up and a good portion of its clientele had left Paris with the exodus of foreigners. Blanqui's paper, *La Patrie en danger*, folded in the middle of December because of lack of funds, while the other radical papers, also short of financial backing, were so badly printed on paper of such poor quality that they were barely legible, although they did manage to survive. But false news and rumors were not diminished in relation to the diminishing paper stock.

Just as the literary diet of the Parisians began to suffer in December through lack of paper provisions, so did their food diet suffer further curtailment during that month. Stocks of food were getting steadily lower, and the pangs of hunger began to gnaw more and more as supplies laid in by foresighted individuals at the beginning of the siege were gradually eaten. But the suffering from hunger was not equally divided.

With a large amount of hoarding and profiteering going on, it is obvious that all those who were able to pay could find everything they wanted in the line of food. With the exception of the dent made in their pocketbooks, the rich did not suffer from famine during the siege. As a matter of fact, the rich and ostentatious gave bigger and bigger feasts simply because food was expensive and hard to obtain. The pleasures of conspicuous consumption were doubled by the ability to eat well at a time when so many people had to eat poorly.

The luxury restaurants seemed scarcely affected by the siege, although they did feature some new and exotic dishes called into being by the difficulties of obtaining more normal foodstuffs. At Peter's, a high-class restaurant in the Passage de Princes, the menus during the middle of December, when most Parisians were eating very sparingly, included, "hors d'oeuvres, two sorts of fish, roast beef, curried fowl, leg of mutton, duck, rabbit, cat, and desserts of prunes and plums." Or take the menu of a supper given at Peter's during the month of December for M. Bonvalet, Mayor of the 3d arrondissement:

> Butter, Celery, Sardines, Olives
> Sago soup with Bordeaux wine
> Salmon à la Berzélius
> Escalloped Elephant Meat, scallion sauce
> Vegetable Salad à la Raspail
> Apples, Pears, Biscuits

Peter's was not alone in serving such meals. Other de luxe restaurants also served the same type of repast, the prices varying according to the popularity of the restaurant.

What was astonishing about such menus was not that the rich were able to obtain so great a variety and quantity, nor even the bad taste revealed by such insolent banqueting when most of the population was starving from hunger, but rather that in the face of such things the populace did not resort to violence either to the diners or to the restaurateurs. So much favor was shown to rich people and good customers that it is indeed remarkable that the people did not break bounds, except occasionally to protest against the slow distribution of meat at the municipal butchershops.

Perhaps one of the reasons why the people did not get out of hand was because no one was absolutely starving, although many people were undernourished. As for the poor, the men were not badly off, but the women and children suffered. The men could get enough to eat, and perhaps too much to drink, merely by enlisting in the National Guard and shouldering a gun. As his home was cold and cheerless, such a man would spend most of his off-duty time in the neighborhood café and bring home nothing to his wife of his daily pay. The wives of these working-class soldiers could not live off their stipend of 75 centimes per day, and they barely kept themselves and their children alive by going to the municipal canteens for soup and to the *mairies* for an occasional morsel of bread. The rationing system, while perhaps good in theory, did not tend toward equality in practice. Although everyone had a card for the meager ration of meat, not everyone had the money to pay the butcher for it. Consequently the poor sold their cards to certain restaurateurs, since their lack of money made the cards useless to them.

It was the petty bourgeoisie, however, who were hit hardest by the rigors of the siege. Most of them were out of work, or their small businesses brought them in nothing. They were too proud or not poor enough to accept charity. But their pocketbooks did not allow them to purchase too much, especially since the prices increased daily. In addition, this class was the chief victim of the adulterated, speculative food products. But they too bore their sufferings without protest, in the hope that these would be contributing in some way to victory over the Prussians.

Furthermore, there was always the hope that science would devise some means of augmenting the food supply, just as there existed the hope that science would be able to invent a new scheme for vanquishing the enemy. The Parisians were assisted in their endeavors to eke out their meager rations by the medical and scientific men of the city, and the discussions in the Academy of Sciences almost invariably turned toward new kinds of provisions and the best way of conserving the old. No part of the animal was wasted at the abattoir: the blood was utilized in sausages; bones were made into *osseine,* a new form of food invented by Frémy; and the fats were substituted for butter. Artificial foods were also invented, the chief of these being artificial milk, devised to stop the increase in child mortality during the siege. Another such artificial and concentrated food was "Of

Meat" (*sic*), of which it was advertised that "a single bottle will give in a few minutes—three minutes at the maximum —the worth of ninety cups of excellent bouillon!" With such an article of diet at their disposal, is it any wonder that the Parisians believed themselves capable of offering a stout resistance?

But even if the Parisians had possessed the means to solve their food problem—which they could not solve—they still had to face the problem of the weather. Not only did the French have to cope with the well-trained legions of Moltke and Roon, but even the elements conspired against them during the siege. Rarely if ever before had the Parisians had to face such severe weather, and never with such limited means at their disposal to combat its rigors.

The bad weather had begun early in the siege. October was a month of heavy rains which made the whole atmosphere gloomy and chilly. As the season wore on the rains turned to sleet and snow. It became so cold that even the hardy winter birds fled Paris—and this at a time when a tiny sparrow would fetch 1 franc, 25 centimes, as an article of food.

During December the temperature was almost always below freezing, sometimes going as low as 15° C. below zero, while the Seine was always covered with ice. This same type of weather continued through January. The succession of rain, sleet, and snow was especially hard on the soldiers in the field and on the women who were forced to stand in queues for hours at a time. However, the soldiers stationed in the deserted villages of the suburbs found it useful to burn the doors, shutters, and furniture of the abandoned houses. This type of "tolerated pillage" sometimes extended to articles other than those necessary merely to keep alive, and this was bad for the morale of the army and even worse for the possessions of the absentees. At any rate, these soldiers did not find the cold so hard to bear as did the inhabitants of the capital, who suffered from a shortage of combustibles.

The extreme cold was aggravated by the lack of fuel, for wood, coke, and gas were at a premium or impossible to obtain. Exasperated by the cold, the poorer people began to cut down trees, snatch benches and fences, and demolish kiosks in order to get fuel. Furniture was broken up to be used for heating, and what was left of the Bois de Boulogne and the Bois de Vincennes was destroyed, as were the trees on the Champs Elysées. Everything that could conceivably burn was utilized, although in many cases the green wood from the fresh-cut trees provided smoke without fire, thus belying an old adage. Here again, as in the case of food, the mayors of the twenty Paris arrondissements neglected pressing matters connected with fuel distribution in order to indulge in political polemics and military criticism. Even the wealthy found it difficult to procure fuel, and the amount the government distributed to the poor was negligible.

Paris was known as a city of bright lights, but the fuel shortage dimmed its illumination considerably. The necessity of conserving illuminating resources caused Paris to undergo a "dimout" during the siege. The cafés had been placed on half-rations of gas, the standard illuminating fuel of the time, and only every other street lamp was lit. The ration of gas was suppressed on November 20, and 20,000 oil lamps replaced gas lights, oil being requisitioned on November 25. Anyone who ventured to use more than his share of illumination or to keep lights burning after certain hours was looked upon as a traitor, especially since the gas was necessary to keep the precious balloon service in operation.

Coldness and darkness were not the only products of the

fuel shortage. Another was a decline in cleanliness caused by the closing of the laundries. Underclothes were not changed very often, and the laundering that could be done with cold water could not fail to be inefficient.

The cold presented another vexing problem—clothing. Although the government distributed some flannel to the needy at the end of the month of December, and the Rothschilds gave to the poor sufficient clothes for 48,000 children, 32,000 women, and 12,000 men, these measures were inadequate, especially since the poorer classes in many cases had most of their clothing in pawn. An interesting aid to the clothing problem was *Flanelle de Santé*, advertised in the newspapers as a protection against rheumatism and epidemics. Shirts of this remarkable, nonshrinkable material could "be worn a consecutive month without ceasing to be comfortable"!

Freezing and starving, the Parisians succumbed easily to epidemics which were more injurious than the actual warfare in terms of mortality. Cold and dampness provided fertile ground for pneumonia and other lung ailments, while diarrhea and dysentery were prevalent because of the bad and inadequate food. Smallpox and cholera were on the increase, and it was estimated that a person's chance of dying from smallpox was ten times that of being killed by a shell. It is no exaggeration to say that the death rate was approximately triple what it was in normal times.

Obviously, there are many factors to account for the increase in mortality, the most important probably being the lack of proper food. With their bodies weakened by hunger and improper diet, it is no wonder that the Parisians fell easy prey to throat and lung diseases as the winter came on. Next to the smallpox epidemic, respiratory diseases were probably the cause of the greatest mortality during the siege.

Other reasons for the increase in mortality can be found in the general unsanitary conditions which prevailed in Paris during the siege. The refugee peasantry who had come into the city, packed into dwellings for the sake of economy and warmth, probably neglected the commonest sanitary precautions and provided a fertile breeding ground for epidemics, much as the farmers from Attica who were crowded together in Athens during the Peloponnesian War gave a great impetus to the plague in the time of Pericles. In addition, the Parisian municipal sanitary arrangements had been curtailed by the siege, as we have seen. Smallpox ranked high among the causes of death in this group of refugees. The epidemic had broken out in 1869 and had abated somewhat in intensity, only to rage anew with the crowding in of the refugees from the countryside and the Mobile Guard from the provinces. Nearly 14 per cent of the deaths during the siege resulted from smallpox, despite energetic action taken by the government making vaccination compulsory.

Not only had the system of sewage disposal been affected by the siege, but the water supply also suffered, and this may have been a contributing factor to the spread of disease. Paris normally used a mixture of Seine water with water brought by means of aqueducts from outside the city. Of necessity, the latter source was cut off during the siege, and the city was obliged to use mainly Seine water. There was a tremendous reduction in the amount of water used during the siege, even the amount of Seine water distributed being only slightly more than half that usual in ordinary times. And a large portion of this water, some of which was used for drinking, was distributed without having been filtered.

The shortage of fuel, which caused the public bathhouses to close, and the shortage of fats for soap for laundering made personal cleanliness difficult to attain. It is no wonder that epidemic and disease were added to the troubles borne by the Parisians during the siege. One point, which is of interest to the general reader as well as the student of medicine, is the fact that women were remarkably exempt from disease during the siege, at least in comparison with men. Of course, infant mortality was high, but, outside of that, the death rate among males quintupled, while it scarcely more than doubled among the females. Given a few more months of the siege, the saving of France would have been perforce left to the women.

Starving, freezing, dying, the Parisian was faced not only with the duty of defending his city but also with the problem of keeping himself alive. Such a situation could not but cause extreme tension among the population, especially when there was a wide disparity in the resources with which people could encounter the dangers of mere existence. And the siege which permeated the atmosphere made escape from its problems impossible. Physically and psychically there could be no escape from the reality of the problems of daily life brought into being by the siege.

Only the stock market seemed oblivious of the great doings which affected the people of Paris so deeply. True, the financial market did respond in trifling degree to various episodes in the war. For example, prices had gone up in the middle of November because of the false armistice rumors caused by Thiers' negotiations with Bismarck, and they had gradually declined after the victory of French troops in taking Orleans. Evidently the speculators calculated that France did not have much chance to win the war, and the quicker peace was made the more favorable it would be. Foreign developments hardly affected the market. The Gorchakov Circular, by which the Russians denounced the Treaty of 1856 which had ended the Crimean War, had little effect upon the Paris Bourse, although this aggressive move on the part of the Russians had caused a panic at London, Vienna, and Berlin.

On another occasion, however, the Bourse seemed to react patriotically for a short time. It exhibited signs of weakness in the middle of December after the French retreat from the sortie over the Marne and the announcement of the retaking of Orleans by the Prussians. But the market soon recovered from this reaction. On the whole, the speculators seem to have taken a long-range view of affairs and to have been relatively unmoved by the exigencies of the moment. The transactions were so inconsiderable and made in such abnormal conditions that it would be impossible to attach any precise significance to any changes that might be noted. The Bourse appeared to be biding its time, waiting for the end of the war, in order to take stock of the extent of the effects of the war upon the French economy. The variations in quotations were so infinitesimal that little of importance can be gleaned from a perusal of the stock transactions during the siege. One fact, however, is worthy of mention: public issues remained relatively firm throughout the siege. The investors had not lost confidence in the financial resources of their government. And if the rest of the population found themselves disturbed over the almost complete cessation of ordinary business and the transformation of what remained to business dealing chiefly with material of war, they could not but be reassured by an advertisement which appeared in the *Journal officiel* of December 5 which indicated that, in the midst of a city fighting for its life, it was still possible to purchase from one A. Huet, with offices on the rue Tronchet, at prices ranging from 13,900 to 19,000 francs, and of weights varying from twelve to twenty tons—steamrollers!

But the government could not face the future with the calm assurance of the stockbrokers and the merchants of steamrollers. Public opinion was such that it could not afford to "sit tight" for another month, as it had done between the end of October and the end of November and wait for events to determine a course of action. Here again the ever-optimistic Gambetta provided them with a cue for further action. Although the Army of the Loire had been defeated and Orleans retaken by the enemy, he did not despair. Instead, he proposed that one part of the Army of the Loire, which had been split by the German action, was to make a rapid turn from a supposed march to the valley of the Rhone and attack the invading Germans on the north of Paris. Gambetta was certain that this movement would be successful, and he advised Trochu that the Parisian defenders could expect aid from the outside armies on December 21.

The government in Paris had no choice but to respond to Gambetta's strategic notions, especially since it had no real plans of its own, and it was determined that a sortie be made in the direction of le Bourget, to the north of Paris. In preparation for this event, the government reclaimed the power of naming the officers of the National Guard, a power which it had mistakenly surrendered at the beginning of the siege for the republican notion of election of officers. The government also ordered on December 18 that the gates of the city were to be closed the next day, thus making certain that the Prussians would realize that some extraordinary military development was pending. The Parisian forces were deployed on December 21, as per the dispatches sent by Gambetta, with Vinoy advancing with 50,000 men toward le Bourget, while General Ducrot led troops to the east in the direction of Bondy. The troops conquered some minor positions, including le Bourget and encamped thereon. But the extreme cold rendered the movement practically inoperative from the start, and the army re-entered its cantonments to await more favorable weather without striking a really serious blow. Even had it not been for the weather, this abortive attempt to break the investing circle would have failed anyhow, for the promised succor from the outside armies did not materialize, since the Germans had succeeded in preventing the army of Bourbaki from marching to the north of Paris.

Suffering from this latest check, it was a poor Christmas for the Parisians of 1870. Even though the government attempted to brighten the season by an extra distribution of rationed food, it could not gain the approbation of the people, who somehow continued to hold their leaders responsible for their plight. Many of the churches did not have their usual midnight Mass on Christmas Eve, because of the lighting and heating difficulties, and the Prussians made the situation no easier to bear by cannonading more fiercely that night, so the noise could be heard throughout the city.

Trochu, perceiving the temper of the population, even offered his colleagues his resignation, which was not accepted. It was decided that the time was not yet ripe for the admission of defeat which his resignation would have implied. A new and last offensive operation must be executed before Paris would be willing to accept surrender. Meanwhile, perhaps, the approach of the traditional New Year's festivities would give the people a respite from the tension of the siege.

Chapter v

While Paris Burns

January 1—*le jour de l'an*—New Year's Day, 1871, the French equivalent of the American Christmas. The day on which everyone forgets his troubles and, true to the spirit of the season, gives gifts in an atmosphere of cheer and good will. But New Year's Day, 1871, is also the one hundred and fifth day of the siege of Paris. Can the people forget the atmosphere of hatred, excitement, cold and hunger in which they have been living for the last few months and revive the spirit of more peaceful and normal times? An effort is made. The government again distributes gifts to the needy; the shopkeepers hope for a return to some normal amount of the regular seasonal trade in gifts. But the siege cannot be forgotten nor laid aside even for one day.

The shopkeepers on the boulevards, who usually did a land-office business in toys during this season, had deserted the toy business in despair. No one had the time or inclination for playthings; the small stallkeepers went in for comforters and revolvers. Toys and candy were no longer the mainstay of the New Year's trade, but rather small articles for the soldiers. The presents did not have to be of an elaborate nature; pieces of cheese and loaves of bread were considered handsome gifts. And a completely new trade, one dealing with war trophies, sprang up. After each combat a certain number of souvenir-conscious soldiers had always brought back some object provided by the enemy from the field of battle. Thus Prussian helmets, sabers, cartridge pouches, and medals were available for a market ready to buy such gifts. But presents such as these were reminders of the siege and did not succeed in making the Parisians forget their difficulties.

Indeed, the New Year was ushered in with more apprehension than delight, because the Prussians were showing signs of a more aggressive disposition in carrying on the siege. By the end of December the Prussians had succeeded in transporting their artillery material and getting their batteries in position, and on December 27 they had begun to bombard the forts to the east of Paris and the plateau of Avron, which they forced the French to abandon. This bombardment continued with increasing intensity to the east of the capital, and on January 5 Prussian siege batteries opened fire against the forts to the south. For the first time the projectiles fell in the interior of Paris.

The beginning of the bombardment of the city itself did not throw the Parisians into a panic. Indeed they had expected it to arrive much sooner than it actually did. During the whole month of October, for example, predictions of the beginning of the bombardment had been made freely. Some newspapers predicted it for October 7; some armchair generals announced its coming on October 14, the anniversary of the Battle of Jena; then it was predicted for October 27, the anniversary of the entrance of Napoleon into Berlin; and others confidently foresaw it for the birthday of King William, of Queen Augusta, of Crown Prince Frederick. But still no bombardment came.

The possibilities of an eventual bombardment took hold

of the public imagination, however, and filled the air with protests and recriminations. The members of the Institute, using elaborate appeals to Grotius, Bluntschli, and other exponents of international law, unanimously "protested against the eventual bombardment of public monuments, libraries, and museums."

Naturally, elaborate precautions were taken for the bombardment. Pictures in the Louvre were packed and sent to the arsenal at Brest for protection, while the "Venus de Milo" was entrusted to the Prefect of Police, who hid it in a vault, using the utmost secrecy. The windows of the Louvre and of the School of Fine Arts were covered with sandbags to protect the treasures that remained within, while Goujon's bas-reliefs on the Louvre were coated with plaster. The "Horses of Marly" by Coustou and the sculptural groups of the Arc de Triomphe were boxed in timber and buried under sandbags, and the treasures of the Luxembourg and the Hôtel de Cluny were placed in safekeeping. At the National Library and the Mazarin Library, precious books and manuscripts were put in the lowest basements, and fire prevention measures were taken. The same procedure was followed with the state and municipal archives. In order that the Prussian shells might bury themselves harmlessly in the dirt, the tiles and flagstones about Sainte Chapelle were taken up, and the beautiful stained-glass windows were hidden by sandbags, turf, and timber supports.

Private individuals were no less careful than public institutions. Already, at the end of September, many had placed buckets of water around their homes in case the shells began falling, and when the bombardment actually started precautions became much more serious. On January 7, Cresson, the Prefect of Police, issued instructions that all combustibles be put underground, that pails of water be kept handy, that the fire department be warned immediately of any fires, that doors be kept unlocked until at least 11:00 P.M. so that passers-by could take refuge if caught in a barrage, and that keys be left with the concierge in case of the slightest absence from the house.

When the bombardment came, its results were much less vicious than anticipated even by the most sanguinary Prussophiles, for it caused little material damage and did not succeed in terrorizing the people. All told, the bombardment lasted twenty-three days, generally from two to five hours at night, averaging 100 shells an hour. Statistics on the effects of the bombardment differ, but the most reliable figures assert that approximately 12,000 projectiles fell on Paris, 1,400 buildings and homes were damaged, about 400 persons were killed or wounded (111 killed outright and 270 wounded), and fifty fires were begun, which were promptly extinguished. Bismarck had set the bombardment for what he called "the psychological moment," but he had miscalculated if he thought it would destroy the Parisian morale or the will to fight. Instead, it strengthened the Parisians in their determination to resist, and the population took the bombardment without terror.

The bombardment struck the left bank first, and it recoiled on the right bank. A long line of carriages and moving vans was formed on the bridges as people attempted to seek safety in the sections that had not yet been bombarded. This emigration from the left bank to the right bank continued during the whole time of the bombardment, following its intensity and progress. These refugees created a housing shortage and a food problem, since they disrupted the rationing system by their movements. They were placed in vacant apartments, just as the refugees from the suburbs had been installed, and some of them went to improvised shelters in the railroad stations or to the barracks of the

Mobile Guard. However, the whole population of the left bank did not move over to the right bank when the bombardment began. Most of the houses and apartments remained occupied, and people took refuge in cellars and basements.

The behavior of the Parisians under this bombardment —almost trivial by twentieth-century standards, but horrendous to the men of the nineteenth century—was symptomatic of the coolness with which the Parisians were able to contain their excitement under certain moments of tension. They had become lax in their bombardment precautions when the shelling did not arrive according to prediction, and they figured that any bombardment would be preceded by a summons to surrender, according to the rules of civilized warfare. So set had they become in this belief that when, on January 5, shells began to fall on the southern portion of the city without any warning, the citizens first believed it to be an error of aiming on the part of the Prussian artillery, an explanation which they found to be eminently satisfactory. But even when it was realized that this was a deliberate bombardment, they were not panic-stricken. If the bombardment had been aimed to terrify and enervate the people, that end was not achieved, for this new common peril inflamed the desires of many of the people to push the resistance to the extreme limit.

As time went on, the Parisians became so habituated to the bombardment that it produced practically no psychological effect upon them, except when nonmilitary objectives and hospitals were hit. Familiarity with the bombardment bred contempt, and it became a topic like the weather, to be discussed whenever friends met, or to be used as an opening gambit in the conversational game, introduced by some such remark as, "The bombardment is rather lively today," or "It's rather slow."

While Paris Burns

The Parisians exhibited great curiosity about the bombardment at first. On Sunday, January 8, practically the entire city went to visit the bombarded sections of the town. They estimated the trajectory of the shells, and street gamins collected the fragments of the shells and sold them for prices between five centimes and five francs, according to the size of the pieces. Indeed, the visit to the bombarded quarters took the place of the peacetime Sunday promenades in the parks.

Of course, the Parisians could not resist the opportunity to turn the bombardment into a jest. Even in the worst days of the siege, some good humor existed in Paris, and the Parisian consoled himself in his hunger by a sally, a caricature, a *bon mot*. There was a superabundance of jests on practically every subject—the Prussians, sorties, rations, and every other item of interest in the siege. The term "psychological moment"—the time which Bismarck had announced as proper for the bombardment to begin—acquired a great vogue. It was said, "I am hungry; it is the 'psychological moment' to set the table."

But this predilection for witticisms did not mean that the Parisians were any the less serious in their will to fight against the enemy. Although Bismarck's attempt at psychological warfare might have no effect upon the Parisians, their own actions conspired to break their morale. The failure of the government to embark on an all-out, full-scale effort to break the siege began to fill some of the Parisians with suspicion. Paris believed that it had the spirit and the means for victory, and there could be but one explanation for the failure of the government to make use of these assets to break through the investing circle. Stories of treason in high quarters began to fill the air, and there was a rumor that Trochu intended to surrender. Trochu defended his military colleagues against the charge of treason and issued a proclamation immediately after the beginning of the bombardment in which he stated that "the Governor of Paris will not capitulate."

In a further effort to bolster the minds and hearts of the Parisians by the hope of victory, Louis Blanc wrote a public letter to Victor Hugo, reaffirming his belief in victory, while Edgar Quinet published an article to the effect that Paris was gaining "a moral victory." These men—Blanc, Hugo, Quinet, and other members of the old republican party, such as Ledru-Rollin—had returned to Paris after the overthrow of the Empire and had used their tremendous moral and literary influence to give tone to the makeshift Government of National Defense, although they too were beginning to show some impatience with its ineffectual tactics.

The continued military inaction of the government was leading to discontent and dissatisfaction, and the dwindling supply of provisions made it imperative that something be done soon if it were to be done at all. The amount of meat in the diet was steadily diminishing, and the horses of the Companie Générale des Omnibus were being requisitioned as a last resort. Even bread had finally to be rationed. Its price had been fixed by decree since September 21, with first-quality bread costing 45 centimes and second-quality 30 centimes per kilogram. These prices remained in effect throughout the siege, but there was a lowering in the quality of the bread. At the end of November the white bread began to degenerate, rice, barley, oats, and straw being added to the flour. The newspapers had to reassure the Parisians that the whiteness of bread was not a sign of its excellence, and that the *pain bis* possessed many health-giving qualities. There was a great hue and cry against those people who fed their horses and pets bread because of the lack of fodder, but the requisitioning of the horses and the disappearance of pets soon put an end to that abuse.

While Paris Burns

At the beginning of January the baking of the first-grade bread was prohibited, and one bakery shop which still continued to make this type of high-quality bread for its luxury trade was the scene of violence on the part of the populace. Finally, in the middle of the month, the government had to forbid the free sale of bread altogether. It was placed on the ration list, and the daily quota was set at 300 grams for adults and half that amount for children. The beginning of the rationing of bread—a staple in the Parisian diet— brought many people to the realization that Paris was on the verge of starvation.

The system of food distribution, now burdened with the addition of bread rationing, was aggravated by the fact that the relief rolls of Paris had swelled from a normal 105,000 to more than 471,000. This was a severe strain on the government's supply of provisions and meant that the state had to resort to more and more requisitions in order to supply the needs of the inhabitants. On January 19 the gratuitous distribution of wine for the needy began; the bakers were made the agents for this distribution. It was also decided to requisition food and fuel from the homes of the people who had left Paris before the siege. Even the conservative members of the government recognized that private property had to forgo some rights in a time of crisis.

And indeed it was a time of crisis. Despite the bombardment, despite the cold, despite the hunger, the people of Paris demanded some action from their military leaders. In despair the government decided on one last try, this time using the National Guard, which was spoiling for a fight. The principal generals of the defense expected little from this last endeavor. At a conference on December 31 some of them, including General Ducrot, had considered any further efforts useless, but others, along with Trochu, felt that since there were provisions for another five weeks and an army of 100,000 men could be formed by incorporating units of the National Guard, it was necessary to make a last effort "for the honor of the country," although admittedly no useful military purpose could be served thereby.

Trochu had been reluctant to lead the National Guard into battle when General Clément Thomas had asked that these troops be given the opportunity to do more for the defense than merely playing the passive role of policing the interior of the capital. Finally Trochu had promised that he would lead the National Guard into battle: "At the last hour, when hunger is pressing on the population and all hope of outside assistance has been abandoned, we will make the supreme effort." Rather a startling statement from a general who should have realized that the supreme effort is best made when conditions are not hopeless, but when help from outside is possible and when the troops have not been debilitated by the rigors of siege life. At any rate, the National Guard, the citizen militia of the people of Paris, was to get its opportunity finally—not because it was believed that they could make any contribution to the defense, but merely because the military leaders felt that they would not listen to reason concerning the capitulation of Paris until some of the spirit had been taken out of them by the loss of blood.

The day chosen for this last desperate sortie from Paris happened to be January 19, the very date upon which King William of Prussia was proclaimed Emperor of Germany at the Hall of Mirrors in Versailles. While France was making this last attempt to save itself, a new German Empire was being created, and one of the acts to which it owed this creation was its success in the humbling of France.

Of course, the sortie was doomed to failure from the beginning. The National Guard were totally lacking in experience and fighting knowledge, just as the generals expected. But one of the reasons for this lack was the fact that the military leaders had never taken them seriously, and, consequently, the professional military men had not devoted the earlier months of the siege to converting them into a capable fighting machine. Had they begun to train these thousands of potential soldiers in the National Guard at the beginning of the siege, it is possible that by January 19 they would have presented a respectable fighting force. As it was, the only fighting quality which the National Guard possessed—and that in ample measure—was spirit. And the underlying purpose of the sortie, at least from the standpoint of the military leaders, was to deprive the National Guard of that spirit.

The National Guard, however, believed itself to be a splendid fighting force, and it had been encouraged in that belief throughout the siege by the newspapers and the military leaders who catered to the public's opinion on such matters. Nor had the National Guard had the opportunity to be disabused of this notion of its fighting prowess until this last sortie, because it was never employed in force until then. Practically all the previous fighting had been done by the regulars and the Mobile Guard, who looked down their noses at these amateur soldiers, as did the generals. Considering the fact that the January sortie had been organized by the military leaders for the express purpose of crushing the spirit of the National Guard and making the population of Paris amenable to the idea of a capitulation of the city, it is remarkable that it did not succeed in that end. For it appears as if the military leaders consciously arranged the action to break the desire for further resistance. If this last sortie is considered as an attempt to break out of Paris, then the military leaders must be condemned for the mismanagement and wantonness which it exhibited. If, however, it is looked upon as a device whereby the National Guard would be led to slaughter and get its fill of bloodshed, then for the first and only time during the siege does the military genius of Trochu shine forth, for he proved himself adept in the killing of Frenchmen if not of Prussians.

The sortie was made in the direction of Montretout and Buzenval with 100,000 men. This was not a weak point of the investment, and the Germans were well entrenched at the points where the attack was made. Nor was any attempt made at a feinting attack in another direction, which might have kept the Germans from sending reinforcements to the spot of the actual attack. The fighting was severe and bloody, and the French did achieve a minor success at first. The Germans quickly recovered, however, and with masses of infantry and heavy reserves of artillery they succeeded in pushing the French back, despite the efforts of Trochu, who exhibited great personal heroism in placing himself at the head of his troops in an effort to stop the German advance. After this setback, the offensive was resumed at nightfall, but the French were unable to hold the heights which they had taken. The unhappy army, which had suffered much bloodshed, was given the order to retreat shortly thereafter, and the troops reoccupied their former positions. Trochu was now ready for the capitulation.

Although this sortie was successful in bleeding the Paris National Guard, Trochu had miscalculated if he thought that this bloodletting would mean a lessening of the desire of the people of Paris to carry on the war or would break their spirit. Instead, the people reacted in exactly the opposite fashion. Even those Parisians who were most ignorant of military matters could not fail to see that the sortie of Buzenval was merely a case of useless bloodshed, and they suspected that there had been sabotage on the part of their military leaders. Actually, this criticism was too harsh, because the generals did not have to sabotage this sortie, doomed to defeat before it started, but their failure in not attempting to make the shedding of blood more worthwhile certainly made them appear treacherous. The general irritation produced by this combat provoked a unanimous cry for revenge, and Trochu was made the scapegoat.

On January 22 the government announced that the office of Governor of Paris was suppressed; General Trochu remained President of the government and the aged General Vinoy, a former senator and supporter of the Empire, took command of the army. The nullity of Trochu as a military commander had finally been recognized; but it was too late to do anything about achieving victory now, and his dismissal came too late to save the government from the expressions of public indignation regarding his mismanagement of military and political affairs. The demotion of Trochu and the change in military chiefs, made to assuage public opinion and alleviate criticism of the government, could not still the insistent complaints. The republican and radical newspapers refused to be misled by what they considered a trick. Trochu had earlier said that "the Governor of Paris will not capitulate," but now the office of Governor had been suppressed; furthermore, the shake-up in government still left Trochu as President, retaining the power but in large measure freed from the responsibilities. To many Parisians this change in commands and the suppression of the office of Governor was merely a face-saving device for Trochu: now that he was no longer Governor of Paris, he would be free to capitulate without breaking the promise which he had given the populace only a few weeks earlier.

Trochu later explained his statement that "the Governor of Paris will not capitulate" by claiming that he meant that he would not give in before any effort of the enemy, but not that he would not surrender before the enfamishment of a city of two million inhabitants. But to the Parisians on January 22, 1871, it looked as though they had been hood-winked by a play on words, as though their government had broken its faith to them and, after leading its men to blind slaughter, now proposed treacherously to sue for peace. Even the conservative papers did not shed tears over the fall of Trochu, feeling that a besieged population had the right to demand that all means of success be exhausted.

Great agitation was manifested in Paris as a result of this series of events. On the night of January 22, the prison of Mazas had been forced, and Flourens and other political prisoners, who had been placed in jail for their participation in the abortive insurrection of October 31, were freed. On the afternoon of the twenty-second, some National Guards of the 101st Battalion, led by Sapia, one of the hottest of Parisian radicals who had advocated overthrow of the government as early as October, marched on the City Hall and attempted to take it. As on the day of October 31, there was already a large crowd gathered in the square in front of the City Hall, peacefully making known their desires to the government by shouting against any capitulation to the Prussians. When Sapia's troops arrived, a delegation was sent into the building to speak to the ministers, but both sides were dissatisfied with these conversations. At the same time, a group of the Mobile Guard from the Vendée came up to the City Hall. These exchanged shots with the National Guard and succeeded in routing them and clearing the square before another group of troops under Flourens could march to the support of the 101st Battalion. By supper time, complete order had been restored in the city, but for the first time during the siege, French troops had fired upon fellow Frenchmen, and five people lay dead and eighteen wounded.

This abortive revolution has often been said to be an

embryonic social revolution, the first engagement of the Commune of Paris which was to follow two months later. Partisans of the Government of National Defense and later historians have pretended to see in this insurrection a movement by the lower elements in society to bring about a social revolution, and they are reinforced in this view by their interpretation of the Commune as a period of class warfare. But a closer examination of the events of the siege leading up to January 22 shows that this insurrectionary attempt was directed against the men of the Government of National Defense, especially their leader Trochu, and not against the organization of society as a whole. For some time, the people had been calling for a new government which would prosecute the war more earnestly, and they were indignant at the mismanagement of the bloody affair at Buzenval. Furthermore, ample warning had been given to the government beforehand, even the conservative newspapers realizing that the people were reaching the end of their rope of tolerance toward what they considered to be the defeatist attitude of the government.

The insurrection of January 22 reveals more planning than the movement of October 31; the followers of Blanqui and the leaders of some of the lower-class National Guard battalions co-operated, although Blanqui himself did not hear about their plans until they were almost ready to go into action. But although the planning was better than that of the insurrection of October 31, the movement of January 22 revealed no more social aim than did the other. It was primarily directed toward maintenance of the defense against the Prussians and opposed to any attempts at surrender, just as the movement of October 31 was. Unfortunately, however, these uprisings had the result of associating the idea of resistance with the idea of disorder in the minds of the conservative bourgeoisie of Paris, even though their chief aim was continued resistance and not social reorganization.

But the bourgeoisie cannot be blamed for misinterpreting October 31 and January 22 and seeing in them the specter of a "red" revolution. Many factors conspired to make such an interpretation seem plausible to them. What was tragic about it was that they proceeded to act upon that plausibility and in so doing plunged France into a civil war, the repercussions of which still exist in France today. The struggle of the people of Paris to achieve victory against the Prussians thus became transmuted into the class struggle manifested by the Commune. This transmutation was achieved during the siege, and the insurrection of January 22 marked one of the steps in the completion of the process by which France was split along class lines.

To understand why Frenchmen in the midst of a war suddenly turned from fighting the Prussians to fighting one another, it must be remembered that under the Empire peace and quiet reigned, and the Emperor did the thinking for everybody. Everything was in its place—the rich in their mansions, the poor in their hovels. Everybody was secure— the rich in their pleasures, the poor in the enjoyment of their sufferings. Despite the benevolent paternalism of the government, the workers were disaffected, but were not revolutionaries in the social sense, being trade unionists and republicans. It was the siege which changed the trade unionism and republicanism of the laborers into what the upper classes thought to be the radicalism of the Communards.

It might be expected that the common dangers and hardships which the Parisians had to undergo during the siege would have bridged the gulf between the classes, and for a time they did. At hearing of the demands which Bismarck had made in his meeting with Jules Favre at Ferrières just as the siege started, the whole population united in a common resolution to resist the Prussians. The newspapers announced that "on the eve of the great battle any division would be not only a fault but a crime" and that "the only urgent question is the welfare of the country: the expulsion of the foreigners."

The editors of the radical newspapers, later accused of conspiring against the defense by their desire to bring about a social revolution, also joined in this movement for unity in the face of the enemy. Blanqui's paper, *La Patrie en danger,* for example, offered its "most energetic and absolute aid without any reservations to the provisional government," with, however, the sole reservation that the government "maintain the Republic and perish with it under the ruins of Paris rather than sign the dishonor and dismemberment of France." Félix Pyat's *Le Combat* also took up this patriotic refrain, saying, "France is above everything." Even Flourens, who was later to be one of the government's most bitter critics, remarked on the unity of purpose manifested at this early stage of the siege, pointing out that the people had absolute confidence in their governmental leaders, asking only that France be saved from defeat and dishonor.

There was every reason to believe that the siege would achieve a new social solidarity. All the people were united in an *idée fixe*—hatred of Prussia; and the mingling of the various classes in the barracks and on the ramparts would certainly fill them with respect for one another. The National Guard, it was thought, would bring about a revolution in mores by binding the people of all classes together in a common cause.

Despite these tendencies making for unity and solidarity, there were other factors working in the opposite direction.

In the first place, although most of the population underwent suffering during the siege, the hardships were not
divided equally. While the upper bourgeoisie suffered very
little from the siege, the lower classes suffered greatly. True,
the proletariat did not suffer so much as did the petty bourgeoisie, for the workers were sustained by their pay in the
National Guard, and their condition was no worse than
usual. But the class in between, composed of the small em-
ployees whose fixed salaries had ceased or were inadequate
to meet the inflated prices, and those living on small
pensions, had no credit at the restaurants and were too
proud to beg or accept charity. They suffered more than
did the laboring masses. But—and this is important—the
actual extent of the sufferings was not the determining
factor; rather, it was the relative differences between the
resources with which the different classes could meet the
rigors of the siege that counted. Food and fuel were at a
premium, and the upper classes were enabled to gain more
of these necessities than were the lower classes. The latter
were embittered at this, while the upper group felt that it
was undergoing relatively more sacrifices than the lower
classes. However, it was a time of crisis, wherein everyone
was supposedly making his best efforts to defeat the enemy.
Since the lower classes felt that they were making as great
a contribution to victory as the upper classes, why should
there not be equality in the distribution of the food and
fuel?

The real dichotomy between the classes, however, lay
not so much in the inequality of suffering undergone during
the hard siege as in the opposing wills to fight manifested
in the different portions of the population. The issue of continuing the struggle had both political and social overtones,
and it played the major role in dividing Parisian society

into two mutually hostile groups. The fact is that the upper classes, for a variety of reasons, wanted the war to come to an end, while the lower classes favored resistance to the last ditch.

The point at stake was not a matter of hatred for the Prussians; both classes were agreed on that. But there were many other reasons why the two groups failed to see eye to eye on the fundamental problem of continuing the war. In the first place, the normal conservatism of possessing classes is such—and this is not confined to Paris in 1870–1871—that any wrench from "business as usual" is looked upon with disfavor. This was especially the case in a war which had lasted longer than expected and thus had taken business away from normal channels for a too-extended period. Furthermore, the possibilities of profit from the war were daily decreasing, while the realities of destruction and suffering were continually increasing. The lower classes, on the other hand, had little property liable to destruction or requisition, and the change from normal business activities and practices had little effect upon them, so they had no inherent dread of drastic economic changes caused by continuing the war. In other words, outside of the danger of the loss of life common to both groups, the lower classes just did not have so much to lose as the upper classes if the war kept going.

Then too, the upper classes did not possess so much faith as the lower groups in the possibility of ultimate victory. Even before the siege had begun, many of the conservative leaders held that further resistance was useless, although they did not dare mention this publicly for fear of the effect upon popular morale. But the differences over the conduct of military operations soon showed the cleavage between the attitudes of the people, red-hot in their determination to carry on the fight, and those of their military and civil leaders, lukewarm in their desire to continue what they were sure was a losing battle.

Of course, the military leaders were right. But this does not mean that the overoptimistic state of mind embedded in the Parisian character during the siege was necessarily a defect. True, the carefully nurtured hopes made disillusionment all the more bitter, but they also kept the Parisian morale high. Although a more realistic appraisal of the military situation would have saved some useless bloodshed and brought the war to a quicker end, the continuance of the struggle, made possible only because the citizens thought they still retained some chance for victory, was to have a profound influence upon the later history of France and even upon conditions during the siege. The immediate effect of continuing the war beyond the point where even daring military strategists would have given it up as hopeless was to cleave Parisian society on the basis of the varying wills to fight present in various portions of the population.

As the sorties from the capital failed and the hoped-for aid from the provinces was not forthcoming, the moderates came to the conclusion that it was best to get it done and over with; but the masses did not see that these failures were inherent in the situation; rather, they tended to blame their leaders for them. Indeed, Paris had reversed the usual situation which exists in besieged towns, where the military power imposes resistance and commands heroism; in Paris, the population demanded resistance and action, and it was the leadership which followed hesitatingly and reluctantly. Jules Ferry, a member of the government, claimed that the sortie of December 21, which was defeated by the intense cold almost before it started, marked the date when the prestige of the military leadership of Paris fell and the population of Paris became hostile to it.

148

The feeling of the bulk of the population can be seen in the National Guard, who were representative of the mass of the people. They believed until the very end in the possibility of a successful defense, but it was not until the final stage of the siege that they were allowed to put their enthusiasm and patriotism to the test at the battle of Buzenval. Left moribund and immobile within Paris during most of the siege, they chafed under their demoralizing inactivity, and it is a tribute to their high morale that they continued in their indomitable will to fight even after the bloodletting of Buzenval.

When the question of armistice negotiations arose, the people also indicated the difference in their attitude from that of their leaders and the upper classes. Not all the partisans of peace had been won over to the idea of resistance to the last ditch after Favre's interview with Bismarck at Ferrières. A large group, not necessarily "appeasers" but people who believed that the war was unnecessary now that the Empire had fallen and that France could obtain nothing from a continuation, felt that peace should be made. The proposal of an armistice in November would have been acceptable to many Parisians, especially to those who valued their stomachs more than a "lost cause" resistance to the Prussians. But the radical republicans would not even think of surrender so long as a Prussian soldier remained on French soil, and so long as there was still a potential defensive force which could be used to drive the Prussians out. As one staunch republican put it, the times call for a "heroic pig-head" rather than a "man of distinction."

Despite the lengths to which the populace was willing to go in order to save itself, it felt that its efforts were going to waste because of the mistakes of the military leaders. Murmurs against the indecision and vacillation of the generals began to be more and more widespread, and criticism was called forth by their defeatist attitude. The soldier could no longer be expected to believe in victory when he no longer believed in his chiefs, but the National Guard men continued to believe in victory for that very reason, since they felt that with a different set of leaders victory would be possible of attainment.

Trochu's proclamation of January 6 that "the Governor of Paris will not capitulate" was an attempt to reassure the people that the government still represented its views. But the citizens had already begun to feel that they had been betrayed and that their leadership was failing them. It is no wonder that the Parisians began to call the government, and especially Trochu, traitors, for the conduct of the siege revealed such incompetence that the people were apt to mistake it for treason.

The charges of treason were not always vague and ambiguous rumors. On January 11 a specific charge was made by certain newspapers that the plans of operations were being delivered to the Germans by the chief of the general staff of the Governor of Paris. Schmitz, chief of the general staff, was probably suspect because of his German-sounding name, but so far as is known there was no treason of this sort during the siege. Nevertheless, the only way the deluded Parisians could explain the fact that the Prussians seemed always ready to counter any sortie from Paris was by reference to treasonable activities. But the important thing to remember is that, whether or not there was any actual treachery during the siege, the people still felt that their military leaders had betrayed them and let them down.

Even the last, desperate, foolhardy action at Buzenval on January 19 was looked upon as a betrayal. The National Guard felt that they had not been given enough of an opportunity to prove their mettle, and the government's request of the Prussians for a two days' truce in order to bury the dead was received by the people with stupefaction and indignation. It seemed to them that the government was attempting to exaggerate the failure of the military action in order to make the Parisians accept more easily the idea of a capitulation in the near future.

But why is it that the lower classes failed to perceive what had been obvious to the military leaders and the conservative upper classes for some time—that capitulation was inevitable? This is because the lower classes had so deluded themselves with the myth of the First French Republic and the great deeds of the Revolutionary Commune of Paris in 1793 that they failed to see that they were putting their faith in words rather than in action. Just as the National Guard, possessing a belief in its own invincibility, refused to be undeceived of this mirage, similarly the lower classes as a whole could not be undeceived regarding their myths. They continued to retain their faith in the *levée en masse*— the arming of all the people—and the name of the Republic at a time when a cooler appraisal of the military situation would have shown that something more than *élan* and "heroic pigheadedness" were necessary if victory were to be achieved.

Another reason why the differences in the desire to continue the war were given a class basis was that the upper classes were, at best, only lukewarm in their attitude toward the new Republic. Victory would have established the new regime beyond a doubt and would have meant a blow to their aspirations for a moderate government denying the egalitarian tendencies traditional in French republican thought and action. The lower classes, on the contrary, were almost unanimous in their strong republican belief. They did not want the cherished Republic for which they had fought so long to undergo the humiliation of a capitulation which would undermine it before its foundations had been fully laid. Thus, to them, any talk of surrender was considered as part of an antirepublican plot, so far did they identify the Republic with France and victory with the Republic.

The lower classes had not wanted to compromise the success of the defense by internal quarrels, but when the hardships of the siege began to weigh on them, and when they thought that the government was not pursuing the defense in the proper manner, they sought for other means to gain victory over the Germans. Even Blanqui had agreed that the first task was to get rid of the Prussians; after that, France's political future could be settled. But when nothing effective had been done to oust the invaders, the masses began to cry: "First the City Hall." After the government had been reorganized along different lines, the Prussians could be driven out with a united and rejuvenated will. The method of political reorganization to be applied was the one which had proved so effective in 1793, when France had been faced with foreign invaders and had driven them out: the organization of the government along communal lines, led by the representatives of the municipalities comprising Paris. This Commune was but a means to the end of defeating the Prussians, and as such it acquired a great appeal for the working class of Paris.

The radicals attempted to point out to the public that the government had betrayed the Republic. The conservative reply was, in effect, "Sour grapes!" based upon the contention that the republican journals had claimed the Republic would save France, but, when it did not, the republican party had disavowed responsibility for what happened. It was obvious, then, that the dichotomy over the will to fight had received a political basis and was no longer a mere theoretical dispute over military strategy.

Aside from the fact that the varying political beliefs usually implied different social and economic backgrounds in France at this time, class distinctions were added to the spirit of party which had begun to make itself felt on the question of the will to fight. The radical and republican political groups favored strong and energetic resistance to the last ditch; the conservatives and reactionaries did not. The lower economic and social classes wanted to fight to the bitter end; the upper classes did not. On the whole, the radical and republican political groups were made up of the lower economic and social classes, and the upper classes were the conservatives, so that the dichotomy between the various classes in Paris, caused by the siege, had both a political and social basis.

There can be no doubt that the fear of the "red specter" on the part of the upper classes dampened their spirit to continue the fight. Besides the dread of a social revolution conjured up by the very word "Republic," the mouthings and behavior of the radicals and neo-Jacobin republicans did not help reassure the propertied classes. The exigencies of the defense had brought about the arming of the populace by means of the National Guard, so that the fear of a radical and socialist uprising was quite real to these timid conservatives, especially when they saw the lower classes become more outspoken and more recalcitrant toward the restraining influence of the moderates as the siege wore on.

Not only did the majority of the military leaders not want to defend Paris because that would have been defending the Republic, but they also feared the Paris mob and the National Guard. General Ducrot even went so far as to accuse them of acting in concert with the Prussians, not realizing that the outbreaks, always following upon the heels of unsuccessful sorties, came as a result of public indignation at the incapacity shown by the military chieftains in those engagements.

The Siege of Paris

The distrust of the masses was not confined to the military heads but could be found among those civilian leaders of the Government of National Defense who were of a moderate stamp. They distrusted the lower classes and believed that it would be best to end the war rather than to continue the struggle with the possibility of an ever-growing socialist movement as a threat to their position. This attitude of "rather Bismarck than Blanqui," the most feared social revolutionary, was to be echoed by the descendants of the French upper classes in the 1930's when the fear of social transformation caused them to say, "Rather Hitler than Blum." The conservative bourgeoisie, the upper classes of 1870, feared that the continuance of the struggle would allow "the Prussians of the interior" to achieve control, with results far more disastrous than if the Prussians without the city were to win the war.

The dislike shown toward the lower classes was also transmitted to their fighting forces—the archrepublican National Guard. Ducrot held that the National Guard was composed of rabble and was of little use as a military force —that it was a positive weakness, in fact, for disorders were a consequence of the universal armament. Many conservatives accepted this view and rallied to the support of the Government of National Defense, even though they considered it too liberal for them, because outside of it they could see only disorganization and discouragement ending in a "supreme disaster."

One of the reasons the conservative upper classes feared a social revolution within Paris was their mistaken notion of what was going on within the radical clubs. They looked upon these clubs as "foyers of sedition" and suspected them of incitement to social revolution. Actually, however, the clubs were not so dangerous as the upper classes thought. At the beginning of the siege, not even the most socially advanced clubs were hostile to the government. As a matter of fact, their firm belief in ultimate victory was a contribution to sustaining the morale of the population, and they also gave the people a chance to "let off steam," an important consideration in a situation as tense as that which prevailed during the siege. In addition, the clubs by their open scheduling of manifestations served to give the government warning of possible uprisings in case those manifestations should turn into revolutionary insurrections, as those of October 31 and January 22 actually did. But despite their value in this connection, the clubs instilled fear into the hearts of the upper classes. Perhaps this was because the clubs gave voice to the opposition to the Government of National Defense and provided a focus for the discontent of the populace, which might otherwise have remained subdued, inarticulate, and unable to find outlet.

In that respect the upper classes were right. The clubs played an important role during the siege, not only because they provided the people with something to do when other forms of entertainment were curtailed, nor simply because they gave the people a chance to air their grievances, but because they did represent an important political force and an articulate public opinion. They constantly gave advice to the government, and it is one of their most characteristic traits that, although their advice was not always easy to follow—in some cases, it was impossible to execute—they would admit of no objection or delay in executing it. The first panacea which the clubs seized upon was Greek fire, but this subject soon became exhausted in the clubs, and it became evident that a more serious and efficacious agent was needed for victory. Then the clubs began to accuse the military chiefs of treason, a cry which became steadily louder as the periods of military inaction alternated with unsuccessful sorties.

But, out of the welter of ideas and suggestions which were spawned in these clubs, there was one proposal which soon acquired predominance and general support among the lower classes: this was the establishment of the Commune. And it was this word which struck terror into the hearts of the upper classes, for to them the Commune meant social revolution and the complete overthrow of the propertied classes and all the traditional values of society. But it is not quite clear what was meant by the Commune to the clubs during the siege of Paris; it seemed to be all things to all men. However, it is evident that to the majority of men the Commune suggested a return to Robespierre and Marat and the Revolutionary Commune of 1793. The Commune was thus a sort of "persistent aggregate" to which the memories of past glories were attached.

Outside of this main idea, however, the Commune meant various and sometimes even contradictory things. For example, at one of the radical clubs in November, an orator spoke in favor of the Commune and also in favor of General Trochu. This is not so ludicrous as it seems; the Commune evidently signified military victory for the speaker and did not imply any social revolution. To another citizen at another club at the end of December the Commune also meant victory, but with the addition of certain monetary changes. He thought that the Commune would exterminate the Prussians by means of Greek fire and high-explosive shells and would then make prosperity reappear by suppressing gold and silver money. To a third citizen, the mere presence of the Commune in the City Hall would suffice to chase out the Prussians. Then, he further explained, the Commune will have need of money and will get it by confiscating the wealth of the clergy, religious congregations, and Bonapartists, followed by the setting up of syndicalist workers' associations to replace the large corporations, especially the railroads.

Perhaps the best explanation of what the Commune meant was given by an orator of the Club Favié in Belleville on January 6, the "reddest" club of the most radical section of Paris: "I wager that even here at the Club Favié, three-quarters of the audience do not know what the Commune is. . . . The Commune is the right of the people; it is equal rationing, it is the *levée en masse,* and the punishment of traitors. The Commune, finally . . . is the Commune!"

While the partisans of the establishment of a Commune were thus not agreed upon its meaning, its opponents were. Everywhere they saw the bogey of the "red" specter, and they believed that the social movement was extremely strong in Paris. Actually, the social movement was very weak during the siege, but its opponents from the upper classes overestimated its strength; they held it to be responsible for the Revolution of September 4 as well as for the insurrections of October 31 and January 22. Some archreactionaries even considered the revolutionary element to be dominant within the inner circle of the government, a view belied by the actions of the government itself.

Not only did the conservatives overestimate the strength of the social movement, but they failed to realize that many of those men whom they accused of inciting revolution were really partisans of resistance to the last ditch, who were willing to hold the social question in abeyance until the Prussians were dealt with successfully. They advocated social changes during the siege only when they felt that the government had betrayed the city and that a better defense could be made under a reorganized government, very much in the same way that Danton had instituted social legislation during the French Revolution in order to strengthen the defensive powers of the endangered Republic. It was the question of resistance rather than that of social change that caused the entente between the government and Blanqui to last barely two weeks; he was so impatient that, by the beginning of October, the inactivity of the government seemed to him a betrayal of the defense. In the same way, the happy accord between the government and Félix Pyat was broken.

It is apparent that the chief reason for the weakness—and strength—of the social movement during the siege is that it was more patriotic than socialistic. All the "socialists"—Blanqui, Délescluze, the members of the Parisian section of the International—were equally ardent in preaching extreme resistance to the foreign enemy. Even though the members of the International subscribed theoretically to the doctrines of Karl Marx, Varlin and its other leaders took a firmly patriotic attitude during the siege, and their acts conformed to those of the advanced republicans. As a result, the question of socialism gave precedence to the problem of the defense of Paris throughout the siege. If the idea of the Commune—which did not necessarily entail socialism—or measures having social repercussions, such as rationing and requisitioning, were advanced in the clubs and newspapers which had sprung up in Paris, it was made abundantly clear that the advantages of those actions were to be found in their contribution to victory rather than in any social gain which might result. When a radical member of the Club de l'Ecole de Médecine attempted to introduce a debate on industrial organization on December 28, the members decided that this was no time to be occupied with the organization of labor, and the debate on social questions was postponed until after the departure of the Prussians.

While Paris Burns

Even had the social movement been more socialistic than patriotic, it probably would not have been much stronger during the siege, for there existed no real or unified conception of what the social movement should be. True, there was apparent unanimity regarding the Commune, but we have seen that the Commune was essentially a patriotic ideal, and that to some people it had no social connotations whatever, while to others it represented varying social arrangements. Indeed, toward the end of the siege, some radicals did not hesitate to state that it was too late for the Commune to be able to chase the Prussians out instantaneously, and that the idea of the Commune must be abandoned. Obviously, to many radicals the Commune was merely a patriotic instrument for victory.

Even the socialism of the most radical Parisian workers, those of the International and of the Federation of Syndical Workers Chambers, was not extreme. When the Revolution occurred on September 4 they had sent delegates to the new government, laying down the following program: immediate election of municipal councils charged with the task of rapidly organizing and arming battalions of the National Guard; suppression of the Prefecture of Police; a declaration in principle of the revocability of magistrates; abrogation of all the restrictive press laws; freedom of meeting and association; suppression of the payments to religious organizations (*budget des cultes*); annulment of all political condemnations and the cessation of all trials for such misdemeanors. These measures certainly did not go beyond any that might be advanced by a nonsocialistic Jacobin or even some moderate republicans, and the government did put some of them into effect.

Nor did the recommendations of the radicals in the so-called Red Posters (*affiches rouges*) of September 14 contain any startling socialistic schemes. The expropriation of food which they suggested might have appeared radical to some timid reactionaries, but it was made clear that this was an emergency measure designed to increase the city's capacity for resistance, and that repayment was to be guaranteed after the war. Later socialist historians have pretended to see in these posters the point of departure for "a complete regeneration of French society," but the posters actually exhibit nothing more than the workers' genuine desire to aid the national defense, and the government eventually found itself forced to execute many of the measures called for in these posters and that did not affect the organization of French society one iota.

The popular mind had no real conception of what the revolutionary movement meant, and even among the men acknowledged to be the leaders of radical thought there was no unanimity in regard to the social movement. The members of the International were tending toward Marxism in their ideology, for Marx had just a few years earlier succeeded in wresting control of the International from the Proudhonians. Blanquism, however, rejected any mass basis; it was Jacobinism flavored with Babouvism and Saint-Simonism. Délescluze and Pyat, two other radical leaders, were straight republican and Jacobin, however. To their ideological differences, Blanqui and Délescluze added personal jealousies, so that there could be very little co-operation between them.

The insurrection of January 22 was a good example of this lack of agreement among the leaders of the Parisian masses. All the left-wing opponents of the government had united on January 6 in issuing a manifesto condemning the "policy, strategy, and administration" of the Government of National Defense and calling for the election of a new government which would be truly representative of the people of Paris, in other words, the Commune. This manifesto was approved by representatives of the International, the moderate republicans of the Union Républicaine, the radical democrats of Délescluze's Alliance Républicaine, the Blanquists, and every other representative of democratic groupings. All sought the means to avoid the capitulation into which they believed Trochu's "plan" was leading them.

But these groups did not all act together in the insurrection of January 22. The Alliance Républicaine was content to post a proposition which it had voted in the preceding evening condemning the lack of decisive measures on the part of the government, the "misdirected action succeeding inertia," and the inadequate rationing program. Pointing out the desire of the populace to continue the struggle until victory, it demanded a Communal government to be based on the election by Paris of 200 delegates to be the sovereign government of France, while at the same time it declared that the republicans wished to avoid the civil war which would certainly result if the National Defense Government persisted in its policy of opposing the will of the people to fight and conquer. The Blanquists, however, were determined to take more energetic action than the mere posting of declarations.

Nevertheless, the movement of January 22 was abortive because of two pieces of news which became known that morning. One was the resignation of Trochu; that appeased the greatest anger of the mob, although some found in it a trick to bring about the capitulation without causing Trochu to lose face, whereas others were willing to wait and see if the new military direction would bring better results. Secondly, the freeing of Flourens from the Mazas prison frightened some of the republican bourgeois; they might have given their aid to a movement to overthrow the "do-nothing or do-it-wrong" Government of National Defense if such a movement had conserved an exclusively patriotic character, but the possible participation of Flourens in such a maneuver led them to believe that there might be a socialist tendency behind the revolutionary attempts. As a result, the insurrection was performed by only one of the many groups hostile to the government, and the government had an easy task in putting it down, a task which would have been much more difficult if the enemies of the government had united.

The failure of this insurrection was indeed a tragedy for the opponents of the government and the partisans of last-ditch resistance. Had they but realized it, there could have been unanimity in their action, because Flourens and Sapia, true to the behavior of most of the radicals during the siege, did not envisage a social revolution as a result of their operations on January 22. Although the fomenters of the insurrection were accused by the government, in a proclamation the next day, of serving the cause of the Prussians, it was really their exasperated desire to chase out the enemy which drew them into insurrectionary activities. In their efforts to substitute a government of victory for one with defeatist tendencies, they succeeded in alienating many of their friends and sending a shudder of horror through the Parisian upper classes by committing the crime of civil war in the face of the enemy.

The insurrection of January 22 of course confirmed the upper classes in their belief that the social movement was strong and dangerous. The government immediately took steps to eliminate this threat by decrees closing the clubs and suppressing Félix Pyat's *Le Combat* and Charles Délescluze's *Réveil*. But the lack of any strong reaction to these decrees indicates the weakness of the social movement. If the clubs were so radical, and if the radical movement were so strong, it might have been expected that strong opposition would have been raised to their suppression; but there was none, which indicates that the government had added another to its long list of miscalculations.

One of the reasons why the social movement was so weak during the siege also lies in the fact that the trade unions, the natural support of such a movement, languished during the war. Inasmuch as many workers had been taken away from their normal occupations to engage in warfare as members of the National Guard, it could not be expected that they would retain their interest in trade union organization. The feebleness of the International during the siege is further proof of this point. The minutes of its meetings show that it was weak, financially and numerically, during the siege; the war had drawn off many of its members, thereby breaking up some of its sections, and it could not even afford to keep a newspaper going. The leaders of the International were conscious of the fact that the workers had temporarily lost whatever interest they might have had in their organization, and that they were also ignorant of its ideology. Its real force lay not so much in its own strength and unity as in the fact that its enemies believed it to be strong and united.

There can be no doubt that the social movement per se, whether Blanquist, Marxist, or any other hodgepodge of humanitarian ideas, was, at the end of the siege, as weak as, or weaker than, it had been at the beginning. The social movement derived what little strength it possessed from its association with the idea of resistance to the last ditch. The lower classes were not so interested in a revolutionary organization of society as they were in defeating the Prussians. If they seemed to take to the idea of the Commune, it was because they thought of it not in terms of a social revolution but as an instrument to be employed in chasing the Germans out of the country, or, after the siege, in destroying that regime which they believed had betrayed the defense of the capital and was about to betray their beloved Republic.

Paris calmed down quickly after January 22, but its resentment was soon at fever pitch again when it learned that Jules Favre had been sent to Versailles to discuss armistice terms. The populace had cried for revenge after Buzenval, and the insurrection of January 22 was but an indication of the lengths to which some portions of the population were willing to go in order to ensure a continuance of the struggle. There were many others who desired another chance to defeat the Prussians but who were unwilling to force an overturn of the government in order to secure this end. Consequently it seemed unbelievable that Paris would choose this moment to capitulate. There was renewed agitation in the capital.

But surrender seemed to be the only course open to the Government of National Defense. Magnifying the strength of the social movement and mistaking its patriotic ardor for socialist zeal, the government feared another outbreak of rebellion from which it might not escape so easily as it had on January 22. Furthermore, the government anticipated the complete exhaustion of the food supplies in the near future, and there were reports of defeats and withdrawals of the French armies in the provinces. While there were rumors circulating in Paris to the effect that Gambetta, arrested in Lille, had tried to commit suicide, or that he had fled Bordeaux and gone to the Army of the North and had been killed there, the government did not subscribe to these, but at the same time it was in possession of news from outside which indicated that the position of France was hopeless. The government felt that, in view of all these circumstances, it could do little else but treat with Bismarck for peace.

While Paris Burns

In opening discussions for an armistice, the government realized that it was risking the outbreak of another insurrection, but it believed that the measures taken after the failure of the January 22 attempt would enable it to deal with an insurrection without too much trouble. The most radical newspapers, which might incite the people to revolt, had been shut down, and the clubs had been closed. But the need for discussing the burning questions of the day as the siege drew to a close was stronger than any governmental decrees, and the clubs again took on their primitive aspect of street assemblies. The boulevards were open, even though the meeting places of the clubs were closed. So people gathered around soapbox orators in the open. There were thus the Club de la rue Drouot, the Club du passage de l'Opéra, the Club du passage Jouffroy, the Club du carrefour Montmartre, and many others. The listeners, standing in the cold, were more excitable and impatient than those of the old clubs had been. Discussions were loud and heated, especially since the orators had to shout above the din of the street noises.

There was plenty to shout about. Some orators demanded the continuance of the struggle; others were willing to accept an armistice but argued about the terms of capitulation; and still others merely voiced general grievances. One of the most common complaints was that regarding food. Inasmuch as one of the reasons given by the government for the necessity of treating with the enemy was the lack of provisions within the city, it came as a surprise to many people that all sorts of food that people had not even suspected of existing began to appear as soon as the armistice rumors began to fly about. This food was brought out of the darkened cellars where it had been hidden and had been saved for profiteering or private use. Prices fell with the rapidity with which they had gone up as merchants hastened to unload their wares in view of the forthcoming armistice. But the reappearance of this food merely served to show the radicals that Paris could have continued to fight against the enemy had the government really wanted to take the stringent measures of requisitioning and rationing necessary for a continuation of the struggle.

The will to fight still lingered in many quarters. This feeling was aided by the fact that most of the population, though it had a passing acquaintance with the Prussian projectiles which fell in the city, had not seen a Prussian during the siege. If the Prussians were not yet in the city, what was the need to capitulate? Some people, such as Emmanuel Arago, a staunch republican, still had the idea of a *sortie en masse,* but this project fell through because they could not get a military leader who was willing to direct it. After all, there were still an army of 200,000 men in Paris and another 300,000 men of the National Guard who were anxious to fight. It would be shameful for them to surrender to famine rather than to a military operation of the enemy.

Even when the firing ceased at midnight of January 26, there were many who did not want to lay down their arms, especially men in the working-class districts. Some of them on the night of January 27–28 decided that they would not give up but, instead, would lead a last sortie against the enemy. On the morning of the twenty-eighth, they beat the drums to call the National Guard to a last violent action, but the government arrested the instigators of this project, two working-class republicans named Brunel and Piazza, and the movement ceased. On January 29, a 21-day armistice was signed at Versailles by Favre and Bismarck. This general armistice, extending from January 31, included all France except the eastern departments where operations were still being carried on around Belfort; it was for the purpose of giving the Government of National Defense time to call a freely elected National Assembly at Bordeaux to decide on the question of war or peace. In the meantime the Germans were to occupy the forts of Paris, and the army, exclusive of the National Guard, was to be disarmed. The city was to be allowed to reprovision itself.

Despite the fact that the citizens knew this armistice was coming, when it actually arrived they felt betrayed and indignant, especially when the *Journal officiel* published the terms of the armistice convention on January 29. Even Veuillot, the conservative Catholic leader, was shocked at this capitulation "which delivers everything," and the indignation of the National Guard knew no bounds. Then began a series of polemics and mutual recriminations as to the conduct of the defense and the actions of the Government of National Defense, the lower classes feeling that they had been betrayed and that the government had actually done nothing to conduct a serious defense or nothing in behalf of the public welfare. Favre and Trochu became the two most unpopular men in Paris.

But it was too late to do anything about it. The city resigned itself to a discouraged defeat, feeling humiliated and dejected. Many newspapers devoted themselves to softening the blow, pointing out that it was not a real capitulation which was at stake and that the newly convoked National Assembly would alone have the right to discuss the conditions of peace with the enemy. Others pleaded with the population to preserve its honor and dignity, especially in the sight of the Prussians who now occupied the forts, and not to allow themselves to degenerate by squabbling with one another. There were some conservatives who took a very optimistic view, holding that the men of

September 4 had saved the honor of France, and that France was even greater in glory and strength than ever before. *Le Siècle,* speaking in somewhat euphemistic terms, said that the enemy "has not conquered Paris at all," and Veuillot's *L'Univers,* presenting the ultramontane explanation for the disasters that had befallen France, blamed the French Revolution for all the evils of the nineteenth century.

The resignation with which the majority of Parisians greeted the news of the capitulation did not mean that all the fight had gone out of them. While the city occupied itself with the problem of reprovisioning, the first food convoys arriving from England on February 4, and with preparations for elections to the National Assembly which was to meet in Bordeaux, the will to fight still lingered. There was a small but powerful minority who were unwilling to accept any peace: Blanqui, for example, writing to Gambetta as late as February 6 exhorting him to further resistance. Even in the large majority which had resignedly accepted the end of the siege there were many who still had their fighting spirit aroused.

For many months the Parisians had lived with the sole purpose of killing someone. Now that the war was at an end and they could no longer kill Prussians, the violent frame of mind continued. The siege had habituated the Parisians to violence. Tempers of the entire population had been quickened by the months in which they had been cooped in with one another and because of the nervous tension which they had undergone. Furthermore, the siege by its necessary dietary restrictions had perhaps impaired the bodies as well as the minds of the inhabitants, and only when psychosomatic medicine is prepared to discuss the effects of mind-body interaction on whole populations as well as individuals will we be able to determine just what effect the physical changes wrought during the siege had upon its psychic manifestations. Yet it is not too venturesome to suggest that the siege had impaired both the minds and physiques of the Parisians, that they had been taken with a sort of "siege fever," and that the nervous strain, the violent habit of mind, and the shortened tempers brought out by the siege could not fail to cause an explosion when mixed together and when the flame of inexpert political maneuvering was applied.

One of the chief manifestations of the growing tension in Paris during the siege was, of course, the increasing class schism which replaced the social unity of the early days of the siege. There could be no reconciliation between the fear, on the part of the upper classes, of the "red" menace and the militant patriotism of the lower classes, determined to gain victory for the infant Republic at any cost. The chasm which developed during the siege between those classes, the "haves" and the "have-nots," was to have significant effects upon the future of France. For the siege made the internecine struggle of the Commune possible if not necessary, and the Communal conflict has been one of the decisive conditioning forces in French history from that day to this.

Chapter VI

Epilogue:
The Paris Commune

Long before the siege of Paris, the lines of cleavage between classes had been set, and the disagreements that arose between September, 1870, and January, 1871, were a manifestation of the gap between social groupings in France which had been gradually widening since the French Revolution.

The upper economic and social classes were of a conservative stamp, and they feared any revolutionary outbreak which might disturb the status quo to their disadvantage. To them, the foundation of a republic involved social disorder and unrest; as proof, they pointed to the Terror of the Great Revolution and the June Days of 1848, which they viewed as an attempt, through violence, to bring about a complete reorganization of society. The lower economic and social groupings, comprising some members of the petty bourgeoisie and the rapidly growing proletariat, were on the other hand staunchly republican. They did not equate a republic with violence and social upheaval, although their notion of a republic did imply social reforms as well as political changes. Their zeal for the Republic had been steadily mounting since 1815 as successive regimes—Restoration, Liberal Monarchy, and Second Empire—had failed to cope satisfactorily with the problems of these "have-nots," so that the "social and democratic Republic" appeared as the only form of government which would respond to their needs and wishes. At the same time, the upper, possessing classes were becoming increasingly suspicious of republican ideology as its social content grew, and they were likewise suspicious of the lower classes who espoused these "red" ideas.

The differences between the upper and lower classes were thus already in existence before 1870. The siege and the accompanying events accelerated the appreciation of the divergences between them and paved the way for an even more violent outbreak of class antagonism in the Commune. Despite the apparent unity that seemed to draw all classes together at the beginning of the siege, the real differences gradually showed themselves until, by the end of the siege, the classes were farther apart than they had ever been before. The dichotomy of the opposing wills to continue the struggle against the Prussians was a faithful reflection of the social, economic, and political distinctions that had grown up between the classes during the course of the nineteenth century.

However, when the siege was over, it might have been expected that class relationships would return to the prewar situation wherein these differences had existed but wherein peace had reigned, at least on the surface. The struggle against the enemy was ended by the capitulation of Paris; the disagreements caused by the opposite wills to fight in the different portions of the population were now of no apparent consequence. Frenchmen should forget that on January 22, 1871, they had begun to shoot at one another, accept the peace which was being forced upon them, and return to normal life while attempting to restore the national economy and spirit after the ravages wrought by participation in a losing war. That might have seemed the logical course of action.

Had the war ended immediately after Sedan with the overthrow of the Empire, such a "return to normalcy" might perhaps have occurred. The Parisians would undoubtedly have been disappointed to see their new government make peace so quickly, but feeling had not yet risen to such a pitch that revolution against the Government of National Defense was to be feared or expected. But in the period from September 4 to January 28 the entire picture had changed: the people had undergone a severe nervous strain and had become inured to violence; a cleavage had occurred in the united front facing the enemy, and class divisions had become apparent even to the point of insurrection. Matters had gone too far for a calm reversion to the past. Instead of a "return to normalcy," the siege had laid the materials for an explosion; the sparks that were to ignite them were struck within two months after the capitulation.

The surrender of Paris did not necessarily carry with it the end of the war. The articles of capitulation merely provided for the surrender of the garrison of the city, the reprovisioning of the capital, and the opportunity to provide for elections in those parts of France not occupied by the enemy. These elections were for the purpose of choosing an assembly that would decide upon the question of continuation of the struggle. Actually, however, the surrender of Paris and the guarantees exacted by the Prussians made the recommencement of hostilities impossible.

This does not mean that the republicans of ardent persuasion were completely ready to give up the battle. There were still three armies in the field, and a good many of the radicals wanted to continue fighting to the last ditch. Blanqui, for example, protested against the signing of a peace even after Paris had capitulated, and many other patriotic radicals felt the same way, especially since they were ready to believe that they had been "stabbed in the back" by the "treason" of the Government of National Defense.

Nevertheless, it was obvious to most Frenchmen that peace was the only possible course. Faidherbe's Army of the North was in a demoralized condition; Chanzy's Army of the West had been defeated by Prince Charles; and Bourbaki (relieved by Clinchart) was fleeing into Switzerland with the remnants of the Army of the East. The possibilities of further resistance were nil, and, even if they had been brighter, the majority of Frenchmen still felt they were not worth the effort and were longing for peace after the disastrous war. France was accustomed to look to Paris for guidance, and the surrender of the capital made further resistance seem meaningless.

The desire of the majority of Frenchmen outside Paris for peace can be seen in the results of the elections to the National Assembly, held on February 8. Inasmuch as the republicans had become identified with the policy of continuing the war, the ground swell of peace sentiment which swept across France after the fall of the capital served to ensure the election of an Assembly composed chiefly of monarchists. Gambetta had been fearful of the election of Bonapartists to this Assembly, which was scheduled to meet in Bordeaux on February 12, and had attempted to proscribe the candidacies of members of that faction. The Paris government had frustrated this attempt of Gambetta to decree the ineligibility of the Bonapartists, and he had resigned. But Gambetta's fear of a Bonapartist menace was unfounded, since the Empire had been completely discredited, and its followers were unsuccessful in the election. However, although the election was carried out in accordance with the principle of universal suffrage, it resulted in the election of a most aristocratic assembly. The political machine of the Empire had been smashed by the war, and Gambetta's policy of defense to the last ditch had so alienated the peasants from the republican groupings that they turned to the landed proprietors of monarchist leanings. Of an Assembly numbering 768 deputies, only about 200 belonged to the republican camp.

These republicans were divided into two main groups: a moderate wing following the moderate republicans such as Jules Simon and Jules Favre, who had been included in the Government of National Defense, and a more radical group that followed Gambetta and that contained many men who, like him, still believed that the war might be continued by making a stand in the Massif Central region and in the northern fortresses while awaiting a turn in the international situation that would cause the foreign powers to intervene in behalf of France. It should be noted that the socialist revolutionaries, the most radical of the republicans, did not succeed in gaining many deputies; even Blanqui failed of election. Instead, the Parisian voters elected the well-known but milder republican revolutionaries of the 1848 period, Louis Blanc, Victor Hugo, Délescluze, and other well-known opponents of the Imperial regime, including Gambetta, Pyat, and Rochefort. Obviously the majority of the Parisians were not thinking in terms of a social revolution, although they were thinking in terms of a radical republic.

The National Assembly opened its sessions at Bordeaux on February 13, 1871, and a government was set up under Thiers. While the majority of the Assembly consisted of monarchists, there was no agreement among these royalists as to who should be king; some of them were Legitimists and favored the Count of Chambord, while the remainder were Orleanists who supported the grandson of Louis Philippe, the Count of Paris. Inasmuch as the royalists were not united and were thus unable to proclaim a monarchy immediately, Thiers became a suitable compromise candidate for the leadership of what everyone expected to be but a temporary government replacing the provisional Government of National Defense. The career of Thiers had been so filled with contradictions that hardly anyone knew exactly where he stood; he was thus able to gain the support of many groups. At the same time, Thiers, playing his cards well, and perhaps seeing here a chance to make good his own claim to power, stated that he would be neutral among the competing groups in the Assembly, and so he was made chief of the executive power.

The immediate task lying before Thiers was the making of peace, and he entered upon negotiations with the Germans at once. In the draft of the treaty which he presented to the Assembly for ratification, there were several items bound to increase the tension that had grown in Paris during the siege and that had not yet had an opportunity to ease off because of the swift flow of political events in the weeks immediately following the capitulation. Outside of the tremendous—for that time—war indemnity and the cession of Alsace-Lorraine, there was also the bitter pill of a German entrance into Paris, a concession which Thiers granted to Bismarck in order to retain the fortress of Belfort for France.

The entrance of the Prussians into Paris, while perhaps gratifying to the pride of the victorious Prussian army, seemed a great humiliation to the people of Paris, who had been fed on stories of their own martial greatness and their soldierly conduct during the siege. Some even thought of marching against the Prussians in an effort to prevent their entrance into the city, or ambushing them upon their arrival. The humiliation of the Prussians' camping in the capital was only one of "the slings and arrows of outrageous fortune" which the Parisian populace thought it had to suffer from a National Assembly whose composition was the opposite of what the choice of the Parisian electorate had been. Although the Assembly ratified the peace at once in order to get the Prussians out as soon as possible, this hasty move could also be interpreted as a desire to submit to the humiliating terms of the peace settlement.

Furthermore, the reactionary measures of the Assembly did much to alienate the Parisian populace. Chief among these measures was the *loi des échéances*—the law on maturities—declaring that all debts, which had been postponed during the war, were to be payable within forty-eight hours, and a parallel measure dealing with rents, which had also been postponed because of the war. This had the effect of throwing almost all the poorer people of Paris, proletariat as well as lower middle class, into immediate bankruptcy, inasmuch as commerce and industry had not yet returned to normal, and nobody had the ready money to pay these postponed obligations. To the petty bourgeoisie who were hit hard by this measure, it seemed to show the dangers of a restoration of monarchical rule, and had the effect of tying them even more closely to their fellow republicans of proletarian background. In other words, these measures helped to cement still further the alliance of lower middle class and proletariat that had grown up during the nineteenth century, for both of them felt that an assembly of landed gentry and upper bourgeoisie was attempting to impose hardships of an undue nature upon them.

These hasty and ill-conceived measures of the monarchist National Assembly thus had the effect of strengthening the radical element within Paris, especially since many of the conservative elements within the city had left Paris after the siege. As Thiers expressed it, the "honest" people had gone forth from the city as soon as the gates were opened to see their families who had been sent to the provinces before the siege had begun and also "to breathe some fresh air." The subtracting of the conservative elements, the wealthier Parisians, from the National Guard made the lower-class and radical element—the "bad part," as Thiers later called it—more prominent.

When, in addition to these disastrous measures, the National Assembly also voted on March 10 to move to Versailles instead of to Paris, the exasperated citizens could see this only as a plot to move the capital away from Paris permanently and to restore the monarchy. When the Assembly then suppressed six newspapers, making the Parisians think that liberty of the press was in jeopardy, and when the government sought to take away the cannon which the National Guard had mounted in strategic spots in Paris, the suppressed feelings of the population erupted. The form which this eruption took was the Commune.

Why did the uprising in Paris in March, 1871, take the form of the Commune? It is unfortunate that the word sounds so much like "communism," for one can be misled into believing that the Commune involved socialist theories in its very name. Actually, this is not the case. The communal idea was an old one in French history and was not necessarily involved in any theories of a new social order. It was primarily a political arrangement which postulated the organization of France on the basis of a federalized organization of communal governments rather than the highly centralized government that had been brought into being by the French monarchy and strengthened by Napoleon I. Under the prevailing centralized system, the inhabitants of the city of Paris had frequently complained that they had no local autonomy but were completely under the thumb of the central government. To a large degree this was true. Under the Second Empire, Paris had been incorporated into the Department of the Seine and was administered by a prefect who was appointed by and was directly responsible to the Minister of the Interior. The executive power of the government of Paris thus did not rest in any official elected directly by the populace, but rather in the hands of the central government itself. This type of administration did not please the city of Paris, inasmuch as it had no control over its budget of municipal affairs, and it is not strange that the citizens proclaimed for their municipal liberties at every available opportunity. This was especially the case whenever the Parisians thought that their interests were being disregarded by the national government in behalf of the provincial areas of France.

While the communal idea itself might refer only to a particular type of political and administrative arrangement, it would be a mistake to claim that no other ideas were associated with it. As we have already seen, the idea of the Commune had certain notions of French glory and victory attached to it from the record of the Commune of Paris in 1793, which had helped to organize the defeat of the invaders of France at that time. The myth of the efficacy of the Commune in being able to repel invasion helped to account for the popularity of the communal idea in Paris during the siege.

In March of 1871 the people of Paris felt that the National Assembly, composed of monarchists who were not in sympathy with the republican leanings of the capital, was seeking, out of suspicion of Paris, to disband their National Guard units and to remove the capital to Versailles. It is small wonder that the cry went up for a federation of autonomous communes as a government for France. Under such a regime the people of Paris would not be brought so directly under the rule of the antirepublican Assembly. Administrative autonomy, as represented by the Commune, also carried with it the myth of the patriotic victory of the Revolutionary Commune, and this represented a high ideal to a populace that felt itself betrayed into defeat.

The lower classes of the Parisian populace—the proletarian and petty bourgeois believers in democratic and social republicanism—therefore turned to the notion of the Commune after being humiliated by the war, by the peace, and by the monarchist Assembly. Of course, rallying to the idea of the Commune was a forlorn hope, but it is characteristic of the Paris Commune of 1871 that it was not provoked by any single, great principle, nor dominated by any single, great leader. Indeed, the Commune was but a vague slogan attracting all the discontented Parisians stirred up by the state of unrest that followed the end of the unsuccessful siege. Perhaps the strength of the Commune lay in the very vagueness of its aims, because it thus served to focus all the subjects of discontent into one stream and unite the disparate elements that went to make up its membership. No one was sure of what the Commune meant; everyone had his own idea, and, on the whole, he felt that it was a good idea—whatever it was.

The composition of the Commune, that is, the men who took the leadership in the newly acclaimed autonomous government in Paris, reveals that it was not the organ of any single class in society, but rather the result of the alliance of the workers and the lower middle class, and, of course, their intellectual leaders—in other words, the very groups that formed the bulk of the support of the radical republican groupings, as opposed to the moderates and antirepublicans. Indeed, many petty bourgeois saw in the Commune an instrument to safeguard the Republic against the threat of the antirepublican and promonarchical Assembly and at the same time to break the strangle hold of centralization on the state.

Now Paris had to undergo a second siege. But this time it was not a united people fighting against a foreign invader. It was Frenchman against Frenchman, the lower-class population of Paris supporting their Communal government against the troops of the conservative National Assembly. Although the Parisians did not have to cope with the problems of fuel and food during this siege, which was of shorter duration than the siege during the war, the bloodshed and destruction were much greater in the civil strife than they had been during the foreign war. Finally the troops of the Versailles government succeeded in retaking the capital and crushing with brutal severity—there was brutality on both sides, including the shooting of innocent hostages—the revolt of the Parisian populace.

Although the Communard government lasted only from March through May, 1871, during the brief period of its existence it did pass some measures of succor for the workers. These, while by no means socialistic, apparently give some basis for the belief that it was a social revolution. Actually, the Commune's first care was its military problem —its own defense against the government troops—and it never had a thoroughgoing social program, any more than did its Revolutionary predecessor. Nevertheless, the Commune had founded itself upon republican and Revolutionary ideals, and inasmuch as these contained notions for social reforms, some students of the Commune have taken the social measures comprehended within the republican ideology out of their context and assumed that the Commune represented a scheme for the social regeneration of the world. This misleading notion was propagandized by Karl Marx and consciously propagated as a part of Communist mythology by Lenin. There is no doubt that ideas of a reformed social order were present in the Commune, but they were present only as part of a larger republican ideal. Yet to many foreigners and conservative Frenchmen, the Commune appeared as a social revolution pure and simple, and certain socialist writers gave added impetus to this belief.

Almost before the smoke had cleared away from the bloody shambles which the Commune had made of Paris, Marx rushed into print with an interpretation of the Commune which painted it as "essentially a working-class government, the product of the struggle of the producing against the appropriating class, the political form at last discovered under which to work out the economical emancipation of labor." [1] The Marxian interpretation became in the hands of Lenin a propaganda weapon which "taught the European proletariat to deal concretely with the problems of the Socialist revolution." [2] In this case, Lenin was being unduly modest, for it was his interpretation of the Commune, rather than the actual events of the Commune itself, which was of "importance for the general proletarian struggle."

This Marxian interpretation is unhistorical because it involves lifting the Commune out of its context in French history and conceiving it as an episode in socialist history occurring in a vacuum. A study of the siege as one of the

---

[1] Karl Marx, *The Civil War in France* ("Marxist Library," Vol. IX [New York, 1933]), p. 43.

[2] "Lessons of the Commune," an address delivered by Lenin in Geneva, March 18, 1908; reprinted in Marx, *The Civil War in France*, p. 81.

events leading immediately to the Commune, and of the Commune itself, brings one to the unmistakable conclusion that it was not, as Lenin called it, "the greatest example of the greatest proletarian movement of the nineteenth century," [3] but rather a patriotic movement of radical republicanism. True, the "neo-Jacobins" and patriots who made up the Commune were composed primarily of members of the lower classes—both proletariat and petty bourgeoisie—but their chief grievance against the members of the upper classes whom they fought was not any complaint based upon their different social and economic standings, but rather an indignation against the manner in which the war had been fought and the humiliation of the peace terms.

Marx interpreted the Commune as class warfare and necessarily socialist because it was proletarian. While it was class warfare, it was not so in the sense implied by Marx. It was a combination of the proletariat and the lower middle classes against the upper classes with their rural allies. Furthermore, Marx made a mistake in believing that the proletariat could fight only for socialism. The Commune was more patriotic than socialistic, but the form which the patriotism took was based on class lines. The siege had generated class hatred, chiefly on the basis of the varying wills to fight; the patriotism of the upper classes did not take the same form as that of the lower classes, who had continued to believe in resistance to the last ditch. The civil war of the Commune was fought primarily on the basis of antagonisms brought to fever pitch by this patriotic issue, and not on the question of changing the ownership of the means of production.

While the patriotism displayed by the lower classes was

[3] Lenin, "Lessons of the Commune," in Marx, *The Civil War in France,* p. 80.

included within their republican ideology, so was their social idealism. Marxists have purged their social theory of any connection with patriotic nationalism or republican political institutions, but the French social movement in 1871 was still compounded of those elements. Only in a laboring class thoroughly imbued with Marxian principles would the proletariat fight solely for socialism; but the French workers of 1871 were not Marxian in ideology, and Marxian socialism did not begin to make any real headway in France until some time after the Commune. In 1871 the French proletariat were closely bound to the republican and social theories that had developed in France during the nineteenth century, and there is no reason to expect them to have acted in a manner which was foreign to their thought at that time. The Commune was indeed a class struggle, but, unlike the Marxian version of class strife, it was a class struggle for ends other than a social revolution, and it was carried on by a lower class that does not quite fit into Marx's category of "proletariat" because it also comprised members of the republican petty bourgeoisie.

One reason why it was thought that the Commune was primarily an attempt at social revolution was the fact that the International gave the movement its support. Indeed, in most conservative quarters, the International was given full blame for the insurrection. In the "red scare" and "witch hunt" that followed the suppression of the Commune, all sorts of fantastic stories were made up concerning the participation of the International in planning and directing the revolt. All the various parties participating in the insurrection were lumped together as part of the International, and the president of the Commission of Inquiry that investigated the Commune even went so far as to state that the International had received 800,000 new members after the end of the siege. Others stated that the International had begun to plot the March insurrection on September 4, while the fell hand of the International was detected in the insurrectionary manifestations of October 31 and January 22 against the Government of National Defense. All this, while highly complimentary to the leadership and spirit of the International, was, as we have already seen, completely untrue. Not only had the International been weakened during the siege, but it did not play the role in the Commune which its enemies suspected. Many of the actions attributed to the International were really not its work at all, but rather those of its adversaries, the Blanquists, who were constantly competing with it for the support of the lower class radicals. However, inasmuch as all dissentient and radical groups were lumped together and classified as members of the International, that organization received the blame, or credit, for all the actions which transpired after March 18.

In the end, not only the International but all liberal and radical movements suffered from the repression following the extinction of the Commune. The Communal insurrection had proved to be a bloody one, and Frenchmen showed themselves much more adept at killing one another than they had been at killing Prussians a few months earlier. The excesses of the revolutionaries, caused by irresponsible individuals, were matched by the excesses of the reaction, which were officially sponsored by a responsible government. The bitterness aroused by these bloody events found vent in a repression that succeeded in hampering the working movement and the republican movement in France for several years.

The Commune and the ensuing reaction thus carried the process of dividing the French upper and lower classes still farther. The Republic, with social implications, still maintained its hold upon the minds of the lower classes.

Epilogue: The Paris Commune

If anything, the reaction may be said to have strengthened the faith of the lower classes in the Republic, for they realized that the oppression was being carried on by a National Assembly essentially antirepublican in attitude. Furthermore, the resistance to the Prussians carried on by Gambetta preserved the patriotic legend of republicanism and connected the Republic with the preservation of the national honor. The actions of the National Assembly thus had the effect of binding republicanism, social idealism, and patriotism more closely together, while the right-wing groups were identified with defeatism, antirepublicanism, and antisocialism.

The gap between the classes, which the siege had helped widen, was thereby increased still further by the Commune. This breach has never been closed; if anything, subsequent events have served to widen it still more, and it has continued to be one of the determinants of French political and social life. Thus the situation in the France threatened by Hitler reflected very clearly the same dichotomy of classes and "wills to fight" that existed in the Paris faced by Bismarck. The events of 1870–1871 reopened the wounds in the French body politic, or social organism, that had been made in 1789 and again in 1848. Those wounds have not yet healed in the France of 1950.

Bibliography

BIBLIOGRAPHICAL AIDS

Maillard, Firmin. *Histoire des Journaux publiés à Paris pendant le siège et sous la Commune.* Paris, 1871.

A list of the newspapers and journals published from September 4, 1870, to May 28, 1871.

———. *Les Publications de la rue pendant le siège et la Commune.* Paris, 1874.

An index of the "satires, *complaintes, canards,* songs, placards, pamphlets, etc." Does not list any material over ten pages long.

Palat, Barthélemy Edmond. *Bibliographie générale de la Guerre de 1870–71.* Paris, 1896.

Alphabetical and analytical index of publications of all kinds concerning the Franco-Prussian war appearing in France and abroad. Magazine articles are listed in addition to longer works.

Quentin-Bauchart, Maurice (Jean Berleux, *pseud.*). *La Caricature politique en France pendant la guerre, le siège, et la Commune.* Paris, 1890.

A catalogue of caricatures.

Schulz, Albert. *Bibliographie de la Guerre Franco-Allemande et de la Commune de 1871.* Paris, 1886.

This has been largely superseded by Palat's work.

OFFICIAL DOCUMENTS, REPORTS, ETC.

Académie des Inscriptions et Belles-Lettres—Comptes Rendus des Séances de l'Année 1870. New Series, Tome VI. Paris, 1870.

Bibliography

Chaper, M. *Rapport fait au nom de la Commission d'Enquête sur les actes du Gouvernement de la Défense nationale.* Versailles, 1873.

A report on the acts of the government from the military point of view. The *Pièces justificatifs* contain correspondence exchanged between the Parisian government and its provincial Delegation, chiefly between Favre and Gambetta.

Comptes Rendus Hebdomodaires des Séances de l'Académie des Sciences. Tome 71. Paris, 1870.

Daru, M. le Comte. *Rapport fait au nom de la Commission d'Enquête sur les actes du Gouvernement de la Défense nationale.* Versailles, 1873.

Enquête Parlementaire sur les Actes du Gouvernement de la Défense nationale, Dépositions des Témoins. 5 vols. Versailles, 1872–1875.

A very important source, but must be used with caution because the witnesses used this occasion to attempt to apologize for their conduct.

Enquête Parlementaire sur l'Insurrection du 18 mars 1871. Paris, 1872.

Lallié, Alfred. *Rapport fait au nom de la commission d'enquête sur les actes du Gouvernement de la Défense nationale, relatifs aux communications, postales et telegraphiques.* Versailles, 1873.

Rainneville, de. *Rapport fait au nom de la commission d'enquête sur les actes du Gouvernement de la Défense nationale.* Versailles, 1873.

Deals with the diplomatic activities of the government.

Rapport fait au nom de la Commission d'Enquête sur les actes du Gouvernement de la Défense nationale, sur les deliberations de ce gouvernement. Versailles, 1873.

Accounts of the meetings of the government.

Recueil des depêches françaises. Ed. Paul Chasteau. ("Documents publiés pour servir à l'histoire de la Guerre de 1870–1871," Vol. VI.) Paris, 1871.

Les Séances officielles de l'Internationale à Paris pendant le Siège et pendant la Commune. Paris, 1872.

Minutes of the meetings of the International. Valuable source.

Séances et Travaux de l'Académie des Sciences morales et politiques. Series V, Vols. XXIV–XXV. Paris, 1870–1871.

CONTEMPORARY AND EYEWITNESS ACCOUNTS

Achard, Amédée. *Récits d'un soldat.* Paris, 1871.

An account of the life of a regular soldier at the outposts.

Adam, Madam (Juliette Lamber, *pseud.*). *Le Siège de Paris; journal d'une parisienne.* Paris, 1873.

A strongly republican account of the siege by the wife of Edmond Adam, for a short time Prefect of Police under the Government of National Defense.

——. *Mes illusions et nos souffrances pendant le siège de Paris.* Paris, 1906.

A reprint of the above work under a different title.

Andréoli, Emile. *1870–1871.* Paris, 1871.

Contains many official documents.

Annenkov, Mikhail Nikolaevich. *La Guerre de 1870 et le siège de Paris; observations, notes et impressions d'un officier russe.* Paris, 1872.

A military analysis by a Russian officer attached to the German headquarters.

Arago, Etienne. *L'Hôtel de Ville au 4 septembre et pendant le siège.* Paris, 1874.

A defense of his actions by the Mayor of Paris from the Revolution to the beginning of November.

Ballue, Arthur. *Les Zouaves à Paris pendant le siège.* Paris, 1872.

Bataille, Alexandre. *Memorial illustré de la guerre de 1870–71.* Paris, 1878.

Bingham, Denis Arthur. *Recollections of Paris.* 2 vols. London, 1896.

Memoirs of an English journalist.

Blum, Ernest. *Journal d'un vaudevilliste, 1870–71.* Paris, 1894.

Bonhomme, Abbé Jules. *Souvenirs du fort de l'Est près Saint-Denis.* Paris, 1872.

Bibliography

Reminiscences of a chaplain attached to one of the Paris forts.

Borchardt, A. *Litterature Française pendant la Guerre de 1870–71*. Berlin, 1871.

Interesting account of the French *esprit* as seen by a Berliner.

Bossaut, Edmond. *Paris pendant le siège*. Valenciennes, 1871.

Bouscatel, Edouard. *L'Impératrice et le quatre septembre*. Paris, 1872.

A Bonapartist account.

Brine, Percival John. *The Revolution and Siege of Paris*. London, 1871.

An uninformative account written by an English pastor.

Brunon, General. *Siège de Paris—Journal du siège du Fort de Vanves*. Paris, 1887 or 1888.

Cadol, Edouard. *Paris pendant le siège*. Brussels, 1871.

A brief and interesting eyewitness account, written before the Commune and, consequently, untouched by prejudices arising from that.

Caise, Albert. *La Vérité sur la Garde Mobile de la Seine et les combats du Bourget*. Paris, 1872.

Caro, Elme. *Les Jours d'épreuve, 1870–71*. Paris, 1872.

Analyses of mental and moral states of Germany and France.

Ceccaldi, T. Colonna. *Lettres militaires du siège*. Paris, 1872.

Military analyses first published in *Le Temps* during the siege.

Cezanne, M. *Relation d'un voyage aéronautique*. Paris, 1872.

An account of a balloon voyage from besieged Paris.

[Chevalet, Emile.] *Mon journal pendant le siège et la Commune par un bourgeois de Paris*. Paris, 1871.

Written by an anti-Communard republican.

Claretie, Jules. *Paris Assiégé; tableaux et souvenirs*. Paris, 1871.

——. *Paris Assiégé, 1870–71*. Paris, 1898.

A reprint of the above, but containing illustrations by Meissonier.

Claveau, Anatole, *Souvenirs politiques et parlementaires d'un témoin*. Vol. I, 1865–70. Paris, 1913.

Clerval, G. de. *Les Ballons pendant le siège de Paris*. 2d ed. Paris, 1872.

Cornudet, Michel. *Journal du siège de Paris.* Paris, 1872.

Cresson, E. *Cent Jours du Siège à la Préfecture de Police.* Paris, 1901.

> Cresson was Prefect of Police from November 2, 1870 to February 11, 1871.

Dalsème, A. J. *Paris pendant le siège.* Paris, 1871.

——. *Paris sous les obus.* Paris, 1883.

> A rehash of the above title.

D'Arsac, Joanni. *Memorial du siège de Paris.* Paris, 1871.

> A mélange of documents, clippings, anecdotes, etc.

Denormandie, Ernest. *Ville de Paris—Le VIIIᵉ Arrondissement et son administration pendant le siège.* Paris, 1875.

> An excellent account of the workings of the municipal administrations during the siege by the deputy mayor of the VIIIᵉ arrondissement.

Dréolle, Ernest. *La Journée du 4 Septembre au Corps Législatif.* Paris, 1871.

> Written by a Bonapartist deputy from the Gironde.

Dreyfous, Maurice. *Ce que je tiens à dire; Un demi-siècle de choses vues et entendues.* Vol. I, 1862–1872. 3d ed. Paris, 1912.

Ducrot, General A. A. *La Défense de Paris.* 4 vols. 2d ed. Paris, 1876–1878.

Dubois, Lucien. *Chapitres nouveaux sur le siège et la Commune.* Paris, 1872.

> Dubois was Inspector-General of the Paris markets.

Du Mesnil, Alexandre. *Paris et les Allemands, journal d'un témoin.* Paris, 1872.

Duruy, Victor. *Notes et Souvenirs, 1811–1894.* 2 vols. Paris, 1901.

Evans, Thomas W. *History of the American Ambulance Established in Paris during the Siege of 1870–1871.* London, 1873.

Favre, Jules. *Discours Parlementaires,* Tome IV. Paris, 1881.

——. *Simple Récit d'un membre du Gouvernement de la défense nationale.* 3 vols. Paris, 1871–5.

Fayard, Jean A. *Histoire de la troisième invasion; Siège de Paris.* Paris, 1871.

Fidus, Journal de, La Révolution de Septembre. 2 vols. Paris, 1889.

Bibliography

Fidus is the pseudonym for Eugene Loudun, originally Balleyguier. Extremely pro-Bonapartist account.

Flourens, Gustave. *Paris Livré.* 3d ed. Paris, 1871.

An important book by one of the most important radicals.

Fulbert-Dumonteil, Jean Camille. *Portraits politiques–Les Septembrisés.* Paris, 1872.

Gambetta, Leon. *Depêches, circulaires, décrets, proclamations, et discours de Leon Gambetta.* 2 vols. Paris, 1886.

[Garnier, Francis.] *Le Siège de Paris, journal d'un officier de marine.* Paris, 1872.

Gautier, Theophile. *Tableaux du Siège, Paris 1870–1871.* Paris, 1886.

Short sketches of Parisian life by a master of French prose.

Goncourt, Jules and Edmond. *Journal des Goncourt—Memoires de la Vie litteraire.* First series, Vol. III (1866–1870); Paris, 1888. Second series, Vol. I (1870–1871). Paris, 1890.

Although both names appear on the title pages, the parts dealing with the siege were written entirely by Edmond, Jules having died.

Gordon, Sir Charles Alexander. *Recollections of Thirty-nine Years in the Army.* London, 1898.

Gordon was a British medical officer attached to the French army as an observer. A very sketchy account of the siege.

Grandeffe, Arthur de. *Mobiles et volontaires de la Seine pendant la guerre et les deux sièges.* Paris, 1871.

Halévy, Ludovic. *Le 4 Septembre 1870, Séances du Corps Législatif et du Sénat.* Paris, 1904.

Harry, Harry. *Guerre de 1870–71, Paris Berné.* Paris, 1872.

Hennebert, Eugene (Major H. de Sarrepont, *pseud.*). *Le Bombardement de Paris par les Prussiens en Janvier 1871.* Paris, 1872.

A full and statistical account of the bombardment's effects.

——. *Histoire de la Défense de Paris en 1870–71.* Paris, 1872.

Henryot, Arnold. *Paris pendant le siège.* Paris, 1871.

Histoire critique du siège de Paris par un officier de Marine ayant pris part au siège. Paris, 1871.

Hugo, Victor. *Actes et Paroles—Depuis l'Exil, 1870–1876*. Vol. III. Paris, 1876.

——. *Memoirs*. New York, 1890.

Johnston, R. M. (ed.). *Memoirs of "Malakoff," Being Extracts from the Correspondence and Papers of the Late William Edward Johnston*. Vol. II. London, 1906.

Johnston was a correspondent for the New York *Times,* using the name "Malakoff."

Joulin, Joseph Désiré. *Les Caravanes d'un chirurgien d'ambulances pendant le siège*. Paris, 1871.

Journal du siège, par un bourgeois de Paris. Paris, 1872.

Kératry, Comte Emile de. *Le 4 Septembre et le Gouvernement de la Défense nationale*. Paris, 1872.

Kératry was Prefect of Police from September 4 to October 13, 1870.

La Baume-Pluvinel, Comte Gontram de. *Le Siège de Paris, Faits et gestes d'un bataillon de mobiles*. Paris, 1871.

Labouchere, Henry. *Diary of the Besieged Resident in Paris,* reprinted from the London *Daily News*. 2d ed. London, 1871.

One of the most interesting and impartial accounts of the siege.

La Roncière–le Noury, Vice-Admiral Bon de. *La Marine au siège de Paris*. Paris, 1872.

Lemelle, Jules. *Siège de Paris, 1870–71*. Orleans, 1871.

Le Verdier, Henri. *Paris assiégé*. Dinan, 1871.

Meffray, Comte de. *Les Fautes de la Défense de Paris*. Paris, 1871.

Michel, Adolphe. *Le Siège de Paris, 1870–1871*. Paris, 1871.

Moland, Louis. *Par Ballon monté*. Paris, 1872.

Consists of letters sent from Paris during the siege.

Molinari, Gustave de. *Les Clubs rouges pendant le siège de Paris*. 2d ed. Paris, 1871.

An important book for the study of the siege. Contains accounts of the meetings of the clubs, most of which appeared in the *Débats*.

Montvaillant, Baron de. *La Garde Mobile de l'Herault au siège de Paris*. Montpellier, 1872.

Bibliography

Murat, Gaston de. *Le Siège de Paris*. Orleans, 1872.

Ollivier, Emile. *L'Empire Libéral, Etudes, Récits, Souvenirs.* Tome XVII, *La Fin.* Paris, 1915.

O'Shea, John Augustus. *An Iron-Bound City.* 2 vols. London, 1886.

A good neutral eyewitness account by the correspondent of the *Standard*.

Paris during the Siege and a History of the Rise and Fall of the Commune, by a Resident. (Captain H. M. Hozier, ed., *Franco-Prussian War*, II.) London, 1872.

Piedagnel, Alexandre. *Les Ambulances de Paris pendant le siège.* 2d ed. Paris, 1871.

Pierotti, Ermete. *Rapports militaires officiels du siège de Paris de 1870–1871.* Paris, 1871.

Contains official reports taken from the *Journal officiel*.

Poinsot, Edmond Antoine (Georges d'Heylli, *pseud.*). *Journal du siège de Paris.* 3 vols. Paris, 1871.

Quinet, Madam Edgar. *Paris—Journal du siège.* Paris, 1873.

Reitlinger, Frederic. *A Diplomat's Memoir of 1870.* London, 1915.

The account of a balloon escape from the siege and a political mission to London and Vienna by Jules Favre's secretary.

Renan, Ernest. *Correspondance.* Vol. I (1846–1871). 2d ed. Paris, 1926.

Rendu, Ambroise. *Campagne de Paris; souvenirs de la Mobile.* Paris, 1872.

Rochefort, Henri. *The Adventures of My Life.* 2 vols. N.Y. and London, 1896.

Memoirs of an important republican radical.

Rodrigues, Edgar. *Blocus de Paris—Opérations militaires de la 2ᵉ armée de Paris et marches de l'Escadron Franchetti.* Paris, 1872.

Rouffiac, J. *Souvenirs historiques sur le siège de Paris et le commencement de la Commune.* Paris, 1874.

Saint-Edme, Ernest. *La Science pendant le Siège de Paris.* Paris, 1871.

Written by the secretary of the Scientific Committee of Defense.

Sarcey, Francisque. *Le Siège de Paris.* 17th ed. Paris, 1871.
One of the most popular accounts of the siege. Written by a journalist of the *Siècle.*

Sheppard, Nathan. *Shut Up in Paris.* London, 1871.
A fairly complete account by an American.

Le Siège de Paris Illustré, par un officier d'Etat-Major. Paris, 1871.

Simon, Jules. *Souvenirs du 4 Septembre.* Paris, n.d.
An apologia by a member of the Government of National Defense.

Taine, H. *Life and Letters of H. Taine.* Ed. E. Sparvel-Bayly. Part III. London, 1908.

Testut, Oscar. *L'Internationale et le Jacobinisme au ban de l'Europe.* 2 vols. Paris, 1872.

Thierry, Edouard. *La Comédie-Française pendant les deux sièges, 1870–1871.* Paris, 1887.
Daily jottings by the general manager of the theater.

Tissandier, Gaston. *En ballon! pendant le siège de Paris, Souvenirs d'un aéronaute.* Paris, 1871.
Interesting and complete history of balloon ascensions during siege.

Trailles, Paul and Henry de. *Les Femmes de France pendant la guerre et les deux sièges.* Paris, 1872.

Trochu, Louis Jules. *Une Page d'histoire contemporaine devant l'Assemblée nationale.* Paris, 1871.

——. *Procès du General Trochu contre MM. Vitu et De Villemessant du Figaro.* Paris, 1872.
Proceedings of Trochu's case against the editors of the *Figaro* for defamation.

——. *Procès Trochu—Plainte en diffamation et outrages envers un dépositaire d'autorité publique.* Paris, 1872.

——. *L'Empire et la défense de Paris devant le jury de la Seine.* Paris, 1872.

——. *Pour la verité et pour la justice.* Paris, 1873.

——. *La Politique et le siège de Paris.* Paris, 1874.

Bibliography

——. *Oeuvres posthumes*. 2 vols. Tours, 1896.

[Vandam, Albert D.] *An Englishman in Paris*. Vol. II. 4th ed. London, 1892.

Vassili, Count Paul. *France from Behind the Veil: Fifty Years of Social and Political Life*. New York and London, 1914.
Vassili was Secretary to the Russian Embassy in Paris.

Veuillot, Louis. *Paris pendant les deux sièges*. 2 vols. Paris, 1871.
Ultramontane polemics.

Villiers, Leon de, and Georges de Targes. *Tablettes d'un mobile*. 2d ed. Paris, 1871.

Vinoy, General Joseph. *Campagne de 1870–71—Siège de Paris —Operations du 13ᵉ corps et de la Troisième Armée*. 2d ed. Paris, 1872.

Vizetelly, Henry. *Paris in Peril*. 2 vols. London, 1882.
Eyewitness account by an English publicist.

Washburne, E. B. *Recollections of a Minister to France*. 2 vols. N.Y., 1889.
Washburne was American Minister to France during the siege.

Wey, Francis. *Chronique du Siège de Paris, 1870–1871*. Paris, 1871.

Whitehurst, Felix M. *My Private Diary during the Siege of Paris*. 2 vols. London, 1875.
Anecdotal account by an English journalist.

CONTEMPORARY NEWSPAPERS AND PERIODICALS

(*September, 1870—January, 1871*)

L'Avant-Garde. Favored resistance to the last ditch.
L'Avenir national. Pro-government.
La Charge. Radical weekly humorous paper, with cartoons by Le Petit.
La Cloche.
Le Combat. Radical journal, edited by Félix Pyat.
L'Electeur libre.
Le Figaro.
Le Français.

195

La France.

La France imposant la paix à l'Europe. Irregular publication of Victor Considérant.

Le Gaulois.

La Gazette de France.

La Guerre illustrée et le siège de Paris. A biweekly.

L'Illustration.

Journal de Paris.

Journal des Débats. Seriously and ably edited.

Journal officiel de la République Française. Official.

Journal des Refugiés. Devoted exclusively to the refugees from the suburbs in Paris during the siege.

Lettre-Journal de Paris. One half of the sheet was left empty for personal messages to be sent to the provinces by balloon.

La Liberté.

La Lutte à Outrance.

Les Mesures de salut public. Irregular publication dealing primarily with the food supply.

Le Moniteur Universel.

Le National.

L'Opinion National.

Paris-Journal.

La Patrie.

La Patrie en danger. Blanqui's famous radical newspaper.

Le Pays.

Le Peuple Français. A conservative paper.

Le Peuple Souverain.

Prédictions sur la guerre. Another irregular publication of Victor Considérant.

La Presse.

Le Rappel. Strongly republican.

La République des Travailleurs. Weekly organ of the Batignolles and Ternes sections of the International.

La Résistance. Organ of the democratic and socialistic *Ligue républicaine.*

Le Réveil. Radical paper edited by Charles Délescluze.

Revue des Deux Mondes.

Bibliography

Le Siècle.

Le Temps. A good source.

L'Univers. Veuillot's ultramontane newspaper.

La Verité.

CONTEMPORARY PAMPHLETS AND POSTERS

(September, 1870—February, 1871)

Budaille, Theodore. *Première Lettre aux vrais Republicains.*
La Crise financière.

Dubois, Frederic. *La Discipline dans la Garde Nationale.* January 1, 1871.

An appeal for stricter discipline in the National Guard.

Le Forçat Evadé, ou Badinguet en rupture de ban.

An attack on Napoleon III.

Guizard, A. *Plan de Bataille adressé à Trochu.*

A "sure-fire" scheme for victory.

Mayer, Cazeau, and Greuier. *La Vote d'Aujourd'hui.* November 3, 1871.

An appeal to vote "no" in the plebiscite of that date.

Montgaillard, P. de. *La Nuit du 31 Octobre.* Bordeaux, 1871.
Written by an eyewitness who left Paris by balloon shortly after October 31 and wrote this pamphlet in December, 1870.

Passedouet. *Suppression des Loyers.* February, 1871.

Pelin, Gabriel. *Réquisitoire contre Trochu, Favre, et consorts.*
Speech at the *club National.* February 26, 1871.

La Question des Abris et la Tactique nouvelle, par un patriote.
December 8, 1870.

A crackpot scheme for protecting advancing soldiers by the use of ambulance mattresses.

La Question des Echéances et la Question des Loyers.

Le Salut de Paris. January 21 (?).

An anonymous handbill telling how Paris may yet be saved by the resignation of the government and the establishment of a new regime headed by Dorian and Ledru-Rollin.

Souvenir du rationnement. February, 1871.

A radical criticism of the Government of National Defense.

Specimen Authentique des infames spéculations auxquelles a donné lieu le siège de Paris. February, 1871.

Union Républicaine Central. *Question militaire.* January 8, 1871.

This Union was founded by the former republican representatives of 1848. This handbill attacked Trochu's military ideas.

———. *Question de Salut—La Répresentation de Paris.* January 9, 1870.

This handbill demanded civil representation in the government, a "courageous offensive," and the "end of treason" in high places.

Les Murailles politiques françaises. 3 vols. Paris, 1873–1875.

An excellent collection of facsimiles of posters of all types. Also contains a very helpful index. Volume I contains *affiches* from September 4, 1870, to March 18, 1871.

Publications Patriotiques de la Garde nationale.

The subjects of these posters include: *La Siège de Vienne en 1683,* by Eugene Gautier; *Au Campement,* advice on how to keep warm and healthy; *Washington,* by E. Farrenc; *Le Siège de Strasbourg en 1870,* by A. Mezières; *Carnot; Le Siège de Venise en 1849; La Santé du Soldat.*

LATER AND SECONDARY ACCOUNTS

d'Almeras, Henri. *La Vie Parisienne pendant le siège et sous la Commune.* Paris, 1927.

An entertaining, factual study, dealing chiefly with the Commune.

Blandeau, H. R. *Patriotisme du Clergé Catholique et des Ordres réligieux pendant la guerre de 1870–1871.* Paris and Angers, 1873.

Bury, J. P. T. *Gambetta and the National Defence: A Republican Dictatorship in France.* London, 1936.

D'Arsac, Joanni. *Les Frères des Ecoles chrétiennes pendant la guerre de 1870–71.* Paris, 1872.

Bibliography

Denis, Samuel. *Histoire contemporaine.* 2 vols. Paris, 1897–1898.

Dayot, Armand. *L'Invasion, le siège, la commune.* Paris, 1901. Notable for its illustrations and pictures.

Duquet, Alfred. *Guerre de 1870–1871—Paris—Le Quatre Septembre et Châtillon.* Paris, 1890. Completely but carelessly documented military and political history.

——. *Guerre de 1870–1871—Paris—Chevilly et Bagneux.* Paris, 1891

——. *Guerre de 1870–1871—Paris—La Malmaison, le Bourget, et le Trente-et-un Octobre.* Paris, 1893.

——. *Guerre de 1870–1871—Paris—Thiers, Le Plan Trochu et l'Haÿ.* Paris, 1894.

——. *Guerre de 1870–1871—Paris—Les Batailles de la Marne.* Paris, 1895.

——. *Guerre de 1870–1871—Paris—Second Echec du Bourget et Perte d'Avron.* Paris, 1896.

——. *Guerre de 1870–1871—Paris—Le Bombardement et Buzenval.* Paris, 1898.

——. *Guerre de 1870–1871—Paris—La Capitulation et l'entrée des Allemands.* Paris, 1899.

Duveau, Georges. *Le Siège de Paris.* Paris, 1939. A good concise military account of the siege.

Fonvielle, Wilfrid de. *Le Siège de Paris vu à vol d'oiseau.* Paris, 1895. Deals with balloons and pigeons during the siege.

Genevois, Henri. *Les Responsibilités de la Défense nationale, 1870–71.* Paris, ca. 1903.

Haristov, Just. *Les Opérations financières de la France pendant la guerre de 1870–1871.* Paris, 1915.

Kelso, Maxwell R. "The French Labor Movement during the Last Years of the Second Empire." *Essays in the History of Modern Europe,* McKay, Donald Cope, ed. New York, 1936.

Koschwitz, Edouard. *Les Français avant, pendant, et après la Guerre de 1870–1871—Etude psychologique basée sur les documents français.* Paris, 1897.

Although well documented, this is really an anti-French polemic.

Landon, Melville D. *The Franco-Prussian War in a Nutshell.* N.Y., 1871.

Mallet, François. *Les Aéronautes, les colombophiles du siège de Paris.* Paris, 1909.

Nass, Dr. Lucien. *Le Siège de Paris et la Commune—Essais de pathologie historique.* 2d ed. Paris, 1914.

This attempted medical history degenerates into atrocity stories against the Prussians.

Palat, Barthélemy Edmond (Pierre Lehautcourt, *pseud.*). *Siège de Paris.* 3 vols. 1898.

Pelletan, Eugene. *Le 4 Septembre devant l'Enquête.* Paris, 1874.

Panorama of the Defence of Paris against the German Armies. Paris, 1881.

Renard, Georges. *Critique de Combat.* 2d Series. Paris, 1895.

Contains a critique of Duquet's writings.

Rouvet, Massillon, *Viollet-le-Duc et Alphand au siège de Paris.* Paris, 1892.

Schloesser, Frank. "Siege Dinners, 1870–71." *The Contemporary Review.* December, 1909.

Taken chiefly from A. Toussenel, *Les Menus d'un Restaurant de Paris durant le siège.*

Tchernoff, J. *L'Extrême-Gauche socialiste-révolutionnaire en 1870–1871.* Paris, 1918.

Villiers, Baron Marc de. *Histoire des Clubs de Femmes et des Légions d'Amazones, 1793–1848–1871.* Paris, 1910.

Deals chiefly with the earlier periods.

MISCELLANEOUS MATERIALS

A. *The Prussians*

Bihler, Otto. *Die Beschiessung von Paris, 1870–71.* Ulm, 1932.

Blume, Wilhelm von. *Die Beschiessung von Paris, 1780–71.* Berlin, 1899.

Busch, Wilhelm. *Das Deutsche Grosse Hauptquartier und die Bekämpfgung von Paris, 1870/71.* Stuttgart and Berlin, 1905.

Bibliography

Herrmann, Otto. *Zur Fräge über die Beschiessung von Paris.* Berlin, 1903.

Heyde, Eduard, and Adolph Froese. *Geschichte der Belagerung von Paris im Jahre 1870/71.* Berlin, 1874.

Joguet-Tissot, J. *Les Armées allemendes sous Paris.* Paris, 1890.

Moltke, Helmuth von. *The Franco-German War of 1870–71.* New York, 1892.

Neukomm, Edmŏnd. *Les Prussiens devant Paris, d'après des documents allemands.* Paris, 1874.

Schubert, Gustav. *Das XII (Königlich Sachsische) Armee-Corps während der einschliessung von Paris.* Dresden, 1875.

B. *Miscellany*

Barbier, Jules. *Le Franc-Tireur; chants de Guerre, 1870–71.* Limoges, 1871.
Super-patriotic poems written during the war and siege.

Dagron, Prudent Rene Patrice. *The Post by Travelling Pigeons.* Paris, 1871.

Défense de Paris. February, 1871.
Anonymous poem telling of the suffering during the siege.

Glais-Bizoin, Alexandre. *Dictature de cinq mois.* Paris, 1873.
An apologia for the Delegation of Tours by one of its members.

Grande complainte de Ratapoil-Badinguet—Histoire veridique de ses crimes et de ceux de sa famille, depuis Romanilli, mère de Badinguet Ier, jusqu'à nos jours.
Contemporary, anonymous poem.

Jacqmin, F. *Les Chemins de fer pendant la guerre de 1870–71.* 2d ed. Paris, 1874.

Leclerq, Emile. *La Guerre de 1870—L'Esprit parisien produit du regime imperial.* 2d ed. Brussels, 1871.

Michelet, Jules. *France before Europe.* Boston, 1871.
Written in December, 1870, this book attempts to present the French point of view during the war. Although written by a well-known historian, prejudice creeps in, so that the book is filled with misstatements, cries of treason and espionage, and recriminations against the Prussians. Michelet's thesis is

that the Prussian victory is merely the forerunner of a Muscovite invasion, that France is attempting to save Europe, and, consequently, the rest of Europe should come to the aid of France.

Millie, J. *Carte historique du siège de Paris*. Paris, 1870.

Robolsky, Herman. *Le Siège de Paris raconté par un Prussien*. Paris, 1871.

An anti-French account by a non-eyewitness.

Viollet-le-Duc, Eugene Emmanuel. *Simple Dialogue pour servir d'introduction au Memoire sur la défense de Paris*. Paris, 1871.

Index

Index

Index

Index

Index

Index

Greek fire, 87-89, 116, 155, 156
Grotius, 132

Halévy, 103
Hegel, 93-94
Hertford, Lord, 67
Horace, 102
Horse meat, 45-46, 105, 136. *See also* Food
Horse racing, 105
Horses of Marly, 132
Hospitals, 23-24, 101. *See also* Ambulance services
Hôtel de Cluny, 132
Hôtel de Ville, 4, 5, 33, 34, 35, 36, 55-59, 69, 99, 142, 152, 156
Housing, 48, 68, 125, 133-134
Hugo, Victor, 9-10, 27, 31-32, 56, 87, 102, 136, 174
Hunting, 42, 43, 105-106

Illumination, 85, 98, 123, 129
Imperial regime. *See* Second Empire
Indo-China, 3
Industry. *See* Business
Institute, 132
Insurrections, 36, 153, 155, 165, 184; of January 22, 142-144, 155, 157, 160-162, 164, 165, 171, 184; of October 31, 55-61, 62, 65, 76, 86, 142, 143, 144, 155, 157, 184
International Workingmen's Association, 85, 158, 159, 160, 163, 183-184
Inventions, 88-92. *See also* Science
Issy, 99
Italian ambulance, 68
Italy, 75

Janssen, 39
Jardin d'Acclimitation, 63
Jardin des Plantes, 63
Jesuits, 73

Joan of Arc, 81, 111
Jouast, 116
Journal des Débats, 115, 116, 117
Journal officiel, 41, 118, 127, 167
Journalists, 28, 50, 82, 113
Journals, 70, 89. *See also* Newspapers
July Monarchy, 1, 11, 171
June Days (1848), 170

Kant, 16

Lafayette, 21, 67
Lavertujon, 41
Ledru-Rollin, 56, 136
Left bank, 133-134
Legitimists, 7, 175
Legouvé, Edmund, 102
Lenin, 181, 182
Letters, 38, 41. *See also* Communications
Lettre-Journal, 116
Levée en masse, 9, 34, 36, 56, 59, 151, 157
Liberal empire. *See* Second Empire
Liberal monarchy. *See* July Monarchy
"Liberty, Equality, Fraternity," 10
Libraries, 104-105, 132
Lille, 164
Lions, 63
Literature, 101
Loi des écheances, 176
Loire, 52
London, 85, 127
London *Times,* 66
Lorraine, 31
Lotteries, 106
Louis Philippe, 1, 11, 20, 175. *See also* July Monarchy
Louvre, 24, 132
Loyd-Lindsay, Colonel, 66
Luxembourg Palace, 24, 132

MacMahon, 4
Magasins du Louvre, 68

Index

Index

Index

Index

Salle de la Rue d'Arras, 86
Salle Valentino, 84
Sanitation, 26-27. *See also* Cleanliness, Public health
Sans-culottes, 79
Sapia, 36, 142, 162
Saxony, 29, 42
Schmitz, 150
School of Fine Arts, 132
Schubert, 91
Science, 87-92, 121
Scientific warfare, 15-16, 88-90
Searchlights, 23-24
Sebastopol, 8
Second Empire, 1-13, 18-22, 35, 43, 52, 60, 72-73, 74, 83, 86, 101-107, 115, 117, 136, 141, 144, 171-174, 178. *See also* Napoleon III
Sedan, 4, 8, 18, 21, 28, 52-54, 113, 172
Seine, 40, 87, 105, 122, 125
Semaphore system, 73
Senate, 5
Seulart, Amélie, 111
Sewage disposal, 26-27, 125. *See also* Public health, Sanitation
Shooting galleries, 106
Siècle, Le, 168
Simon, Jules, 105, 174
Sisters of Charity, 69
Skating, 105
Slackers, 69
Smallpox, 124-125
Snow sculptures, 104
Social classes. *See* Bourgeoisie, Classes, Proletariat
Social evils. *See* Alcoholism, Gambling, Prostitution, Vice
Social movement, 157-164, 182-184. *See also* Classes, Proletariat, Radicals, Republican ideology, Socialism, Socialists
Social revolution, 58-61, 143-145, 153-157, 160, 162-163, 170, 174, 180-183. *See also* Class schism, Class struggle, Classes, Radicals, Social movement
Social solidarity, 144-145
Social structure, 147-149, 185. *See also* Bourgeoisie, Classes, Proletariat
Socialism, 158-162, 177, 180-185. *See also* Republican ideology, Social movement
Socialists 153-154, 159-160, 164, 174, 180-181. *See also* Proletariat, Radicals, Republicans
Sorties, 32, 35, 54-55, 58, 94-97, 113-114, 118, 127-129, 138-143, 148-149, 150, 153, 166
Speculators, 26, 127. *See also* Bourse, Business
Sports, 105-106
Spy hunt, 49, 50, 99
Steamrollers, 127
Stock market. *See* Bourse
Strasbourg, 10, 31-34, 37
Strategy, 81-83, 94, 124, 128-129, 137-140, 152. *See* Gambetta, Government of National Defense, Trochu
Suburbs, 22-23, 26, 42, 68, 99, 116, 122, 133
Sufferings, 146-147, 152. *See also* Classes, Morale, Psychology
Suicides, 111-112
Sumner, Charles, 13
Surrender. *See* Capitulation
Swiss, 43
Switzerland, 173

Temps, Le, 115
Théâtre-Français, 101-103
Theaters, 101-106
Thiais, 35
Thiers, 20-21, 52-55, 58, 61, 65, 126, 174-175, 177
Thomas, General Clément, 80, 95, 138
Timbre, 115

Index